Planning & Remodeling
Family Rooms, Dens & Studios

By the Editors of Sunset Books and Sunset Magazine

Lane Publishing Co., Menlo Park, California

Acknowledgments

We wish to thank the many architects, designers, and homeowners whose ideas and experiences contributed to this book. A special thank you goes to David Putnam.

Staff Editors:

Anne K. Turley
Alyson Smith Gonsalves
Julie Anne Gold
Barbara G. Gibson

Design:

Mark Landstrom

Illustrations:

Clyde Foles

Front cover:

Small, but packed with activities, the family room on the cover offers study space, conversation area, and a hard-working storage and display wall, plus storage under the built-in seats. For another view, see page 30. Architects: Pennington & Pennington. Photographed by Jack McDowell.

Editor, Sunset Books: David E. Clark

First Printing October 1979.

Contents

Cozy den
Looking down from a loft, you see how much can be packed into a tiny area without losing the illusion of uncluttered spaciousness.
Architect: Ernst Meissner.

Add an Activity Area

Ways to gain space for family rooms, dens, studios

"We need ten more rooms for all the things we love to do!" That's a common lament, as energetic people crowd more and more activities into small spaces and busy schedules.

You may want extra room at home for anything from a craft to a second career, not to mention making music, painting pictures, challenging your pinball machine, exercising to keep fit, meditating to keep sane, running a home business, sewing, refinishing furniture, developing your own film, or pursuing any number of other do-it-yourself projects.

All those extra activities that take home life beyond the basics of eating and sleeping seem to require extra space. But they don't always require separate rooms. With creative planning, a house can contain enough activity areas to satisfy the most multitalented, high-energy family. After all, your home may be a beehive of industry, but you probably don't want it to look like a beehive, with a separate cell for every activity.

for general ideas before turning to the special-feature sections that focus on important considerations like lighting and storage.

The first chapter, "Family Rooms" (starting on page 10), looks at areas that, by nature, serve many purposes: conversation, relaxation, playing games, watching TV, listening to music. More casual than living rooms, family rooms are gathering centers. Like scrapbooks, they contain the mementos of shared experiences, reflecting the personalities and preferences of their owners.

Many of the family rooms shown have a seating area at their core, with activity areas surrounding the conversation center. A stage for musical performances, children's play areas that keep toys out of the main traffic paths, desk areas, game tables, craft centers, combination family room / kitchens — these are just a few of the multi-use areas that are neatly blended into family rooms.

While you may not discover the precise remodeling plan for your family room, you'll be able to pick

(Continued on page 6)

Shop for ideas

The rooms in this book fall into three major types: family and recreation rooms for gathering people together; retreats, dens, studies, and home offices for activities that flourish where there's some privacy; and studio areas tailored to special equipment for arts and crafts. You'll probably want to skim through the photographs and shop

Multipurpose garage conversion

Transforming an attached garage into this high-beamed, window-lined family room opened up the entire house. Beams hold loft for play or quiet retreat. Family can enjoy games at the game table, gather near woodburning stove for cozy conversation, or invite friends for a party in this casual but visually striking family room. Design: Gary Tuchman.

Take life easy in a den

Warm-toned wood paneling, a cheery fire, and comfortable seating add
up to mellow den atmosphere. Pivoting TV, mounted on pull-out drawer, is
part of an entertainment center that is housed behind cabinet doors.
Lights recessed above bookshelves aid book selection.
Architects: Goodwin Steinberg Associates.

Studio loft with an eye-filling view

An inspirational loft setting for art work, this home
studio has dramatically angled window wall.
Tracklights augment the abundant natural light. For
easy clean-up, there's a sink on the other side of the
wall partition. Architect: Clement Chen.

...Continued from page 4

and choose among the many adaptable ideas in
this chapter. For example, a new arrangement of
your furniture may make room for an additional
activity area. Or a way to combine kitchen and
family room may inspire you to expand two rooms
into one multipurpose space.

Even more casual than the family room, the
recreation rooms highlighted in "Playrooms for
Adults & Kids" (starting on page 32) show ways to
create space for such spirited activities as gym-
nastics, fitness exercises, pool, pinball, and just
plain horsing around. The time-honored basement conversion to "rec" room takes on an up-
beat, up-to-date look that is as functional as it is
attractive.

The chapter on "Quiet Corners" (starting on
page 46) takes you away from the commotion of
group activities and into calmer territory for privacy. There are sitting areas off master bedrooms
and lofts for getting above it all, as well as cozy
nooks, window seats, and hideaway corners, all of

which turn unused or wasted space into delightful living areas.

Places for reading, study, and paperwork do not have to be totally secluded. A desk tucked into the kitchen or family room may be all you need. We've selected working-at-home situations for the chapter on "Dens, Studies & Home Offices" (starting on page 54) that display excellent organization, good lighting, and versatile storage. Whether you want to add a desk to your family room or transform an extra bedroom into an office, you'll find ideas to adapt for your home.

"The Arts at Home" chapter (starting on page 74) covers "wet," potentially messy arts and crafts, as well as "dry," relatively neat pursuits. We'll show you how to create studio space that can complement your talents and enhance the time you spend painting, weaving, making ceramics, crafting jewelry, or making holiday ornaments. You'll see how work space — sewing areas, darkrooms, workshops—can be tailored to special equipment and activities. Your particular craft may not be covered, but the design principles are adaptable: storage is flexible and plentiful, arrangement of equipment simplifies the work flow, lighting makes work easy on your eyes, and the flooring is compatible with the work at hand.

Start planning

The first step in planning is to evaluate your needs. A survey of your indoor activities (beyond the basics of eating and sleeping) will help you arrive at a list of priorities that, ideally, includes something for everyone. An easy way to start your survey is to make a home activity chart with these eight headings: *Activity, People Involved, Equipment, Furniture, Lighting, Storage, Time Spent per Week, Permanent or Fad?*

The last heading may cause some controversy— your youngster may insist her devotion to playing drums is eternal and deserves a special platform in the center of the family room. But it's wise to avoid built-ins for kids, since a desperate need for space to play drums can change overnight to an equally desperate need for a display area for skating trophies. Where youngsters' activities are concerned, versatility is the word to live by.

After completing your chart, note which activities are group oriented and which need only semiprivacy. Also note any pursuits — sculptural welding, for example — that require isolation because of noise, smell, or mess. The goal is to combine as many compatible activities as possible into one area.

Directing traffic

Few things are as annoying as the patter of feet through the middle of a conversation or activity area. To avoid this, you must establish good traffic patterns at an early stage in your planning.

How many different pathways do people follow when walking from one part of your house to another? Are you happy with the patterns that exist? If you rearrange a room, what effect will that have on the traffic patterns? Ideally, traffic should flow *to* rooms, not *through* them. Moving a door or channeling traffic by rearranging furniture may solve the problem. A rough sketch of the layout of your house, with doorways and traffic flow indicated, will help you plan traffic routes to accommodate new uses of space.

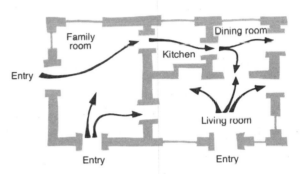

Awkward traffic flow brings people through the middle of activity areas.

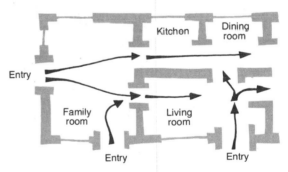

Corrected by moving doors, traffic flows along sides of rooms out of activity areas.

Options for remodeling

Ingenuity applied to your present rooms may take you far, so evaluate the existing space before deciding to add on or move out.

Do you have a formal living room that stands abandoned while the whole clan crowds into the kitchen eating area for conversation and play? Perhaps you could change the living room into a family room. And if that room is next to the kitchen, you might want to remove a wall to make a large multipurpose area.

There are lots of possibilities. Do you have an extra bedroom? It could become a sewing room, guest room, study, den, home office, craft area, or retreat. Redesigning storage and lighting and splurging a bit on a new decor may be all that's needed to bring your present family room or recreation area up to date. An unused attic or basement can be finished off. A porch or patio can be filled in. A garage can be converted to living space, workroom, or studio. All of those options are less costly than adding a new room or radically changing the structure of your house. But don't proceed willy-nilly. You probably will have to consult a professional for some or all of your project.

The discussion on these two pages concerning removing a wall or converting an attic, basement, porch, patio, or garage will not tell you how to do it yourself. It *will* give you an idea of the kinds of problems you'll be facing. Once you're acquainted with the general difficulties, you'll have a better notion of what portion of the remodeling you can undertake by yourself and what portion will require professional help.

Don't forget that a permit is required for virtually any change of use or change of structure. Check local building codes and ordinances to find out what is legal. There are different rules for habitable rooms (family rooms, living rooms, bedrooms) and nonhabitable rooms (studios, workshops, kitchens, baths, storerooms). If an attic, basement, or garage fails to satisfy the legal requirements for a family room, you may be able to convert it into a studio or workshop.

For additional information on building, remodeling, and home decorating, you might want to consult some of the other *Sunset* books listed on the back cover.

Removing a wall

You frequently read about removing a wall to open up a room—and it sounds so simple! Sometimes it is, but you can't wave a magic wand and make a wall disappear. Here are some questions and problems you must deal with before you tear down a wall.

Is the wall load bearing? That is, does it carry part of the weight of the house? All exterior walls — and usually interior walls — that run perpendicular to the ceiling and floor joists are load bearing. Removing a load-bearing wall is not impossible, but it is a job for a professional. And if there are wires, pipes, or heating ducts in the wall,

whether it's bearing or nonbearing, you're likely to need professional help to remove the wall and reroute the wires or pipes.

Attic conversions

The desire for space compels many home owners to cast hopeful eyes upward — toward unused space in the attic. But before you become too involved in daydreams of converting your attic to living space, consider the difficulties you'll have to overcome if your attic was not built with expansion in mind.

Does the attic have enough headroom? Code requirement for ceiling height in a habitable room (living area, as opposed to workshop or storeroom) is 7-1/2 feet over at least half of the usable floor area. You'll need adequate headroom at the top of the staircase, too. An architect or contractor may be able to suggest practical solutions if your attic is too low.

Can the structure bear the extra weight? Consult an architect or contractor to be certain the foundation, bearing walls, and existing attic floor joists can support added weight.

What about flooring? The attic "floor" may be nothing but bare joists and the lower story's ceiling. In that case, you'll have to lay a subfloor before putting down flooring or carpeting.

Don't forget about insulation and ventilation. And while you're making a list of things to consider, be sure to include electricity, heating, plumbing, and soundproofing.

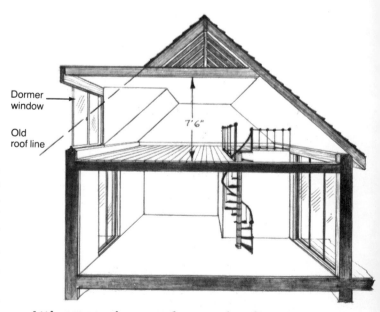

Dormer window

Old roof line

7'6"

Attic conversions need proper headspace
Adding a dormer window may give you the required ceiling height in the attic.

Porch & patio conversions

Turning a framed porch into an extra room may be a relatively simple matter of replacing screens with windows. Turning a brick patio into living space, on the other hand, may be as much work as adding an entire new room. The less structure present in the porch or patio, the more challenging your remodeling project will be.

Even if the porch has an adequate foundation, you still may have to deal with building up the floor, installing insulation, supplying ventilation, plus bringing in electric circuitry, heating ducts, and possibly plumbing. And you'll want to finish the exterior to match the house.

Patio conversion is more difficult than porch conversion. The foundation may not be up to code, and if it isn't, you'll be virtually starting from scratch and adding a new room.

Basement conversions

If you're lucky enough to have a basement area with headroom of 7-1/2 feet, you could be the proud owner of a basement recreation room such as those shown on pages 34 and 35. If the basement's ceiling height is below code, perhaps you could plan for nonhabitable space, such as a workshop or studio.

Dingy walls, exposed wiring, heating ducts, and plumbing pipe, not to mention problems with leakage, seepage, and condensation—you may be faced with some or all of these when converting a basement to usable space. Problems with water are the ones most likely to require professional advice and assistance. You face a leakage problem if there are cracks in the masonry walls or concrete floor. You have to deal with a seepage problem if water is soaking into the pores of the masonry. Waterproofing the inside of the basement without eliminating excess water in the ground around it probably will not cure the trouble.

Air is normally humid, and when humid air hits the basement's cool masonry walls and pipes it condenses, creating yet another common moisture problem. A vapor barrier and insulation with vapor-barrier backing are among the solutions. You can prevent condensation on pipes by winding insulating wrap around them.

Once you've solved the water problem, then finishing the floors, ceilings, and walls will be comparatively simple. As in other converted areas in a house, adding electricity, heating, and plumbing in a basement may require a professional.

Garage conversions

Do you leave your car in the driveway because your garage resembles Ye Olde Junque Shoppe? If so, you've solved one of the major problems of converting a garage—you've found another place to park your car.

A garage can be converted to anything from a family room to a workshop or studio. A workshop or studio is not considered habitable space and therefore doesn't require ceiling height of 7-1/2 feet. For a family room or other living area, be sure you'll have enough headroom once you've finished the floor and ceiling.

Major tasks ahead of you—for either a separate or attached garage—include removing the garage door and framing in a new wall for that side, upgrading the floor, reinforcing the structure (if necessary), installing insulation, waterproofing exterior masonry walls, putting in electricity, and possibly adding heating and plumbing. You may need to provide a new doorway for access between garage and house, and you may want new windows, as well. Don't forget to plan for finishing the interior walls and ceiling. And some exterior finishing may also be in order.

An attached garage can be easier to convert than a separate one because wiring, heating ducts, and plumbing are nearby.

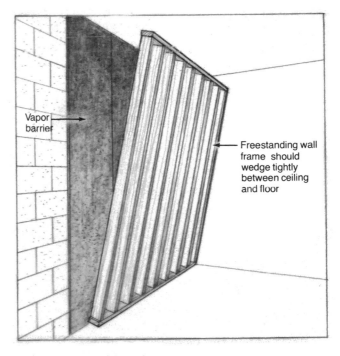

Vapor barrier

Freestanding wall frame should wedge tightly between ceiling and floor

Install a vapor barrier
Sheets of foil or plastic film between the masonry wall and a freestanding wall frame can eliminate condensation problems.

Family Rooms

This is where we live

Laughing, talking, playing, or just lounging—the family room is the place where home life grows. By nature it's a multipurpose area: somewhere for the kids to dump out all their blocks and build a city, a place to read quietly, watch TV, play cards and board games, show slides, flip through the family album and laugh at how funny we used to look. The family room can also be called on to double as an entertaining center, eating area, sewing room, guest room, study.

At worst, a family room is where you put the old couch and TV and let the kids bounce around. At best, a family room harmonizes the different interests and activities people like to share.

In this first chapter we offer ideas ranging from grand clan-gathering places to intimate family areas tucked into limited spaces. Most of the rooms were remodeled from existing space; some were added on; some are new.

The theme of the rooms on pages 11 through 19 is versatility. You'll see how various families have solved the problem of bringing adults and kids together in a casual but orderly atmosphere.

From pages 20 through 23, you'll find examples of the popular family room / kitchen combination, followed by sections on lighting, family rooms converted from patios, and a garage that became a spectacular split-level family lodge. Small and cozy family rooms bring this chapter to a close.

Sketches of the floor plans are included to show you the overall arrangement of a room. You'll also find special features on storage (pages 16 and 17), skylights (pages 18 and 19), and artificial lighting (pages 24 and 25).

Family rooms are partly private souvenir shops, and each reflects the lives and tastes of its owners. We wouldn't be surprised to hear that you had shopped through the ideas in this chapter and found a shelf system from one room, a fireplace from another, a color scheme from a third, and put them together to make a family room uniquely yours.

You'll find that the main feature of most of these family rooms is the seating area. Note that each seating area has a focal point—often the fireplace. When you begin planning your new family room, these features should be among your first considerations. Additional spheres of activity, such as a play area for kids, room for a game table or desk, or space for a special hobby should not interfere with the conversation area. Remember that traffic should be planned with access *to* your seating arrangement, not *through* it.

Kids' stuff—so near & yet so far
The conversation pit provides a calm oasis with focus on a towering fireplace chimney. In the foreground is space where children can play without intruding in the seating area. The *ficus benjamina* grows out of a built-in planter; you can just see the game table behind it. Architects: Moyer Associates.

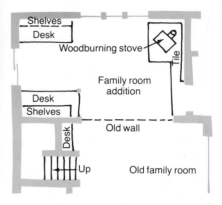

Satellite areas for crafts and study
Just off the main seating area, three desks offer enough work space for crafts and study. They're far enough away from the conversation area to provide privacy, but open enough so youngsters who use them don't feel isolated. Architect: Ernst Meissner.

Playroom in the family room
This children's play area is self-contained even though it's right next to the conversation pit (also shown on page 11). Storage closets hide toys and games. A bookcase running the length of the room holds a children's library at this end, grown-ups' books at other end. Architects: Moyer Associates.

Plan for versatility

Your 10-year-old wants to work on model airplanes, your teenager wants to watch TV, you want a quiet place to relax—and everyone wants to be in the same room. How can a family room handle all the demands made on it?

Defined zones keep everyone together but out of each other's way when you congregate in the family room. The four rooms shown here illustrate zone-planning. Each has a unified appearance but contains much more than a main seating area.

Changing the floor level is one way of defining activity zones. A conversation pit establishes boundaries within a room. So does a raised stage. A window seat, loft, alcove, or a desk placed away from the core of the room also let you have privacy and community at the same time.

Furniture arrangement and lighting can help break up the room. Instead of one large grouping, cluster the furniture into a core area and a smaller, intimate setting. Walls can be put to work to keep TV, stereo, books, and display shelves in one central area, freeing the rest of the room for other activities. Use recessed lights, track lights, or pendant fixtures to beam down see-through borders for different zones.

Provide a focal point for the main seating area. A fireplace, wall hanging, window, or storage system will make the area more relaxing by offering people something to look at. And the room will gain its character and overall atmosphere from whatever you choose as a dominant feature.

Music reaches new heights

Elevated on its own stage, the organ overlooks this plush-carpeted conversation pit. Children love to dive off and roll down the seating area; overnight guests sleep on it. Architects: Churchill- Zlatunich - Lorimer.

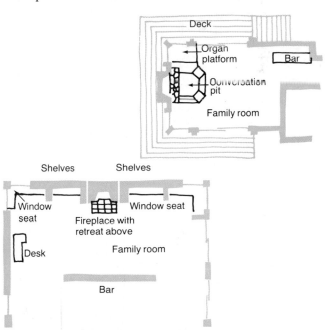

Disappear up the ladder

Like an enclosed loft, a small retreat perches above the fireplace. (The chimney is really behind the hide-away.) Elegantly detailed built-in storage conceals stereo speakers. Recessed downlights accent the top shelf, while soffit lights play up the richly paneled ceiling. Desk and window seats add more quiet zones to this handsome family room. Architects: Ellmore/Titus.

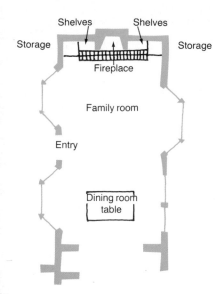

Come sit by the fire

Designed as a single unit, the fireplace and storage shelves are recessed in the wall. A smaller picture over the fireplace would look out of place, but the large picture with its fresh primary colors is perfect. You can sit on the elongated hearth and select a book from the shelves; the cushions match the couch and chairs. To the left, a cabinet conceals the TV. Notice how the couch and table create a room within a room, dividing the family room from the dining area. Architect: Francis Palms.

Blue portholes peer over hearth

Bold wood paneling extends up the arched chimney and across the ceiling, dominating the structure of this family room. Everything works together, but nothing quite matches: the stained-glass portholes are slightly different and the storage systems are asymmetrical. The cabinet to the left of the fireplace holds a TV; on the right, plush blue cushions invite you to relax with a book. Two ceiling-mounted spotlights accent the entire hearth area. Architect: Robert Peterson. Stained-glass: Peter Mollica.

The family hearth

Central heating notwithstanding, the hearth is still the heart of many homes. The psychological satisfaction of gathering friends and family around a toasty fire remains undiminished.

Most of the family rooms in this book have fireplaces — some rather grand, some more modest. There are even a couple of woodburning stoves that provide the main source of heat for the room, as well as gratification for the psyche.

As a focal point, the hearth naturally draws the central seating around itself. Everyone likes to look at a dancing fire. And even when the flames have died, the hearth can sustain interest. You may want to hang artwork on the chimney, perhaps with a spotlight to emphasize it. Or use the mantel as another place to set artwork.

Storage and display shelves on either side of the fireplace reinforce it as the focal point. Just make sure they enhance the shape of the hearth and the architecture of the room. You needn't group art objects symmetrically in the display shelves, however. Sometimes the most visually pleasing wall systems have shelves placed at irregular intervals. Whatever your solution, treat the hearth and nearby wall area as a unified space. The hearths on these two pages may give you some inspiration.

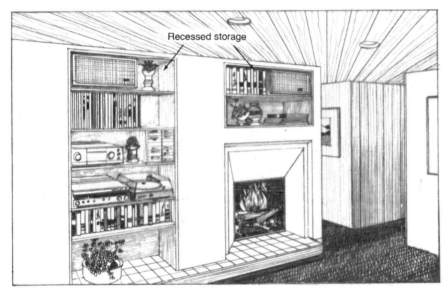

Recessed storage

The clean-lined modern look
Impressive, large fireplace has well-integrated built-in storage shelves above and to one side. Even the stereo speakers on the top shelves seem to match the rectangular look of this hearth-wall. Fireplace and shelves are bordered with wood trim. Recessed lights in the wood-paneled ceiling brighten the elongated tiled hearth. Architect: E. Paul Kelley.

Hearth rounds out a corner
Like wings extending from the rounded chimney, bookshelves carry out the horizontal lines of the mantel. Located in the corner of the family room, this fireplace has inlaid tiles and a hearth that lengthens into built-in seats. Design: Peter Van Dyke.

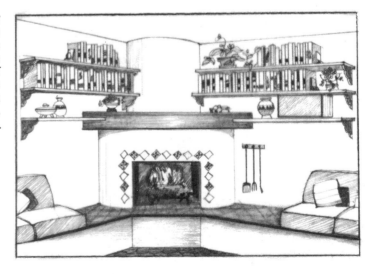

Family room storage

If your family room looks like the family toy box, it's time for some fresh storage ideas. New storage units for books, magazines, board games, stereo, television, and other belongings can bring order to the family toy box without intruding on the casual, friendly atmosphere of the room.

Two considerations enter into the planning for your family room storage. First, you'll need to decide which items you want stored out of sight and which you want kept in view. Families with youngsters may want some special storage for toys, and family rooms that do double duty as guest rooms, party rooms, and study areas will have some particular requirements. But for the most part, items used by the family as a whole pose most of your family room storage problems. You may want to hide the TV, toys, and games, yet keep books and art objects displayed on open shelves.

Second, you'll want to evaluate the room to find the best location for the new storage so it blends with the structure of the room. Any extensive system, especially one that shows off lots of rich wood, tends to dominate a room. While smaller, freestanding systems don't draw the eye as much, they should also fit into the overall room design.

The horizontal lines of a mantelpiece, window, or molding may suggest the height for a storage system. If your fireplace lacks a mantel but has a prominent chimney, you may want to follow the chimney's vertical lines, adding storage all the way to the ceiling. Lines made by unusual angles shouldn't be broken — it's better to fill the entire angled area with storage than to have two conflicting lines.

You'll find more storage suggestions in the special sections on art supply storage (pages 80 and 81), and bookshelves (pages 60 and 61), and the *Sunset* book *Ideas for Storage.*

Fabric panels hide clutter

Jumbles of games, photo albums, and magazines in open cupboards cause that messy toy box look in the family room. An easy way to hide the clutter is to make stretched fabric panels that fit snugly into the cupboards. Construct the frames from fir 1 by 2s trimmed to fit inside open cupboards, with 1/8 inch to spare all around. Stretch and staple fabric to the frames, and attach small ribbon tabs to the tops. Then simply wedge each panel into place. To open, pull on the ribbon tab. Use a boldly printed fabric, if the room needs an accent, or coordinate the material with the draperies or upholstery. Architect: Homer Delawie.

Pivoting guest bed

A storage system that doubles as a guest room? It's possible with a pair of Murphy beds mounted on pivoting wall units. As storage, the units include cabinets, bookshelves, and a desk. When guests arrive, the shelf and desk areas spin to reveal the pull-down single beds attached to their backs, complete with framed pictures. When pulled down, the beds rest on hinged legs. Lights swing down for reading and up when the beds are stored. The cabinets double as small clothes closets with shelves on top for bedding. Architect: Philip Dinsmore.

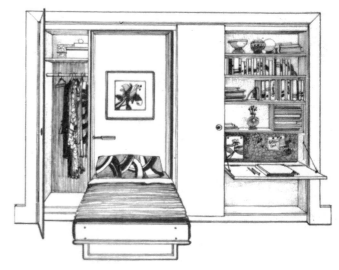

Divider stores TV

Does the blank eye of a turned-off TV make you feel as if Cyclops is staring at you? You can avert its gaze by storing the set in a low room divider like this. The TV slides out on a tray and sits on a ball-bearing lazy Susan, so it can swivel to face viewers almost anywhere in the room. The support tray rolls on metal drawer glides; a 1-inch aluminum tube reaching to the baseboard helps brace the tray when it's extended. You could mount a similar slide-out system in a wall storage unit, as long as the unit is stable enough to bear the weight of the TV when it's pulled out. Design: Lawton Shurtleff.

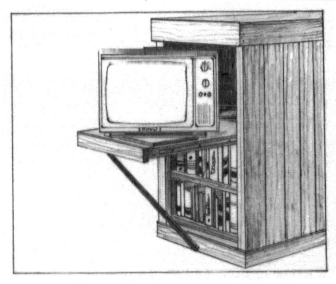

TV behind push-down panel.

Six-way storage

An ingenious example of space-saving storage, this wood-paneled, freestanding unit performs a number of functions. On the bottom, a large bin for firewood hides behind a collage of log ends. Lower the panel in front of the center section and you have a pivoting television on a pull-out platform. The panel is mounted on spring-tension sash window tracks. Above the television there's a bookshelf and display niche. Diagonal paneling used over the entire unit makes a handsome background for a picture. At the very top, you can show off your favorite plants. Architect: Ken Himes.

Magazine rack

Keeping magazines orderly but accessible is a problem. One solution is to build a magazine rack. The one shown is glued and nailed together, then nailed to the trim of a small wall section. You could build a vertical row of racks and store children's magazines on the lower racks and adults' periodicals higher up. Architect: Russell V. Lee.

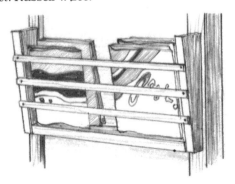

Let the sun shine in

You can transform a dull, dim family room — or any room — into a dramatic, sun-filled area by adding a skylight.

Skylights come in a variety of styles and can be installed with different shaft angles to direct light where you want it. Use a small skylight to illuminate a reading nook or highlight a sculpture, a large one to diffuse light throughout a room.

Acrylic is the most common skylight material. It's available in clear sheets (for overhead views) or translucent panels (to reduce glare and diffuse light).

Where sunlight is intense, hot spots on floors can be avoided if you select skylights with built-in shutters, use insulated double domes, or block light below the shaft with horizontal curtains or shutters. Installing a translucent panel beneath a skylight shaft at the ceiling line is another way to diffuse light; it also controls heat loss.

On these pages you'll see some of the skylights available for home installation, as well as different skylight adaptations.

Through a skylight thinly
A single, skinny skylight brings an illuminating strip of light to a reading corner.
Architect: William Simpson.

Light shaft angles

Shafts tunnel in light when there is space between roof and ceiling. Here are some samples of various shaft angles.

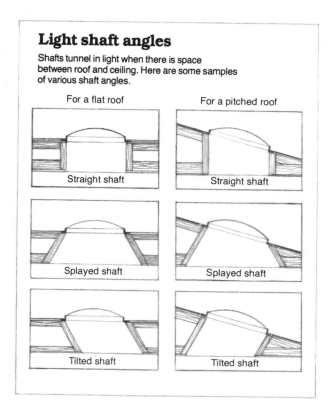

For a flat roof — Straight shaft
For a pitched roof — Straight shaft
Splayed shaft
Splayed shaft
Tilted shaft
Tilted shaft

Skylights for home installation

These are the most common models and the simplest to install yourself.

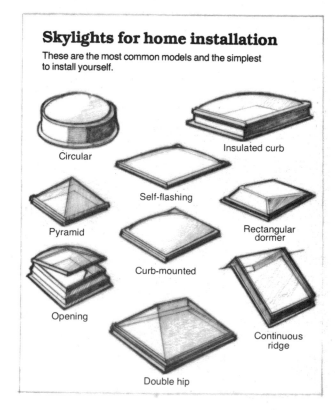

Circular
Insulated curb
Self-flashing
Pyramid
Rectangular dormer
Opening
Curb-mounted
Continuous ridge
Double hip

Through a window wall

Light and spaciousness are shared by the rooms on each side of this dramatic window wall. The skylight over the raised, tiled spa also seems to belong to the adjacent family room. Such lavish use of glass creates a Moorish courtyard atmosphere. Architects: Cobb and Morton.

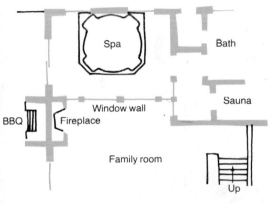

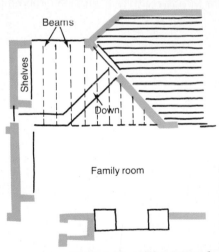

Through ceiling panels

Light pours into a music alcove off the family room through bronze-tinted, tempered skylight panels placed between structural beams. While accenting the trapazoidal shape of the alcove, the panels bring the outdoors into the entire area. Architect: E. Paul Kelley.

A wraparound family room

When the owners approached the architects for a family room addition, they had more than a few special requests. They wanted lounging room for their family of six; a way to enjoy the fireplace and watch TV at the same time; yards of storage and shelving for collectibles, craft material, books, and kitchenware; a desk area; and—oh, yes—a place for a stained-glass window made by a talented neighbor.

What the architects developed is the radiant wraparound family room shown below and on the next page. The kitchen, once an ordinary pullman type, is now the core of the room. A wide seating platform joins the U-shaped kitchen counter under a trellis of vertical grain Douglas fir.

The trellis creates a cozy, sheltered, indoor gazebo. It also visually defines the activity areas in the open room. On one side, the family room shown below has space for a couch and game table. On the opposite side (not shown), a wall of storage cupboards extends along the far side of an eating area. The fireplace (shown on the facing page) is one of the few remaining features of the original structure.

Architects: Moyer Associates.

Comfort zone seating
Wide seating platform invites you to curl up with a book or chat with the cook. To the left is a lounge area used for family activities and entertaining—it was once a breezeway. Large, clear globes on dimmer switches offer versatile lighting.

Cook's-eye view

Cook takes center stage in this trellis-covered kitchen surrounded by the family room. From the work counter the cook can enjoy the fireplace, TV, and stained-glass window while keeping track of family activities on three sides. Shelving that flanks the fireplace is on adjustable tracks.

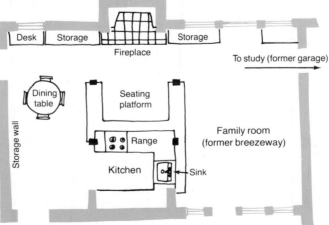

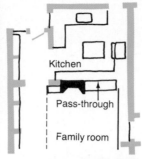

Open or closed, as you choose
Open the louvered folding doors and you have a handy pass-through for family snacks or party nibbles. Close them and the pass-through seems part of the fireplace wall. Architect: Donald K. Olsen.

Kitchen

Pass-through

Family room

Semi-open
One of the most versatile walls in the house, this divider not only has a large pass-through but also houses built-in stereo speakers. Lighted by three surface-mounted downlights, pass-through functions as counter and bar for casual entertaining. Architects: Goodwin Steinberg Associates.

Kitchen

←—Pass-through

Family room

Completely open
Separated only by dining table and ceiling-hung kitchenware, the family room and kitchen form a single, charming room decorated à la Provence. Architect: Robert Stoecker.

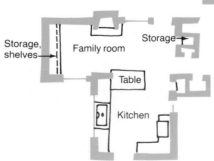

Storage, shelves

Family room

Storage →

Table

Kitchen

Close to the kitchen

"Hey, somebody bring me a sandwich!" you shout from the deep recesses of the family room couch. Snacks and lounging in the family room seem to go together. And the closer you are to the kitchen, the more likely you are to persuade someone else to fetch your sandwich.

Family rooms near the kitchen are handy for reasons other than proximity to the peanut but-ter. For one, the cook can keep an eye on family activities and not feel left out. For another, you can plan casual parties and not miss any of the action while popping hors d'oeuvres into the oven.

Family room and kitchen can be one large open area, or partially separated by a divider or pass-through. Large pass-throughs can serve as eating counters or bars; small ones can be fitted with shutters and closed off.

The family room/kitchen combinations on these pages offer a range of ideas from a com-pletely open floor plan to a small, closable pass-through. But no matter how closely you bring the rooms together, don't be surprised if your request for a sandwich is still met with, "Go get it yourself! And while you're in there get me a..."

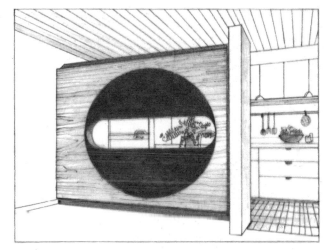

Hand it through the slot
Cut out of a high divider, this modernistic pass-through looks like a gigantic mail slot. It adds conveni-ence, as well as bold graphic appeal, to both kitchen and family room. Architect: Wendell Lovett.

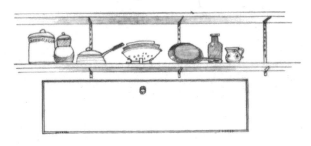

Open or shut pass-through
Opened and suspended by chains, the hinged pass-through acts as a shelf for plants and dishes. Closed and held in place with a deadbolt, it blends into the wall. Architect: Rodney Friedman.

Window on the family room
Once a patio, the family room now uses the former outside window as a pass-through from the kitchen. Architect: David B. Gilchrist.

Artificial lighting

You don't have to be a Broadway director to stage dramatic lighting. Spotlights, floodlights, downlights, track lights, wall washers, dimmers — these are just some of the fixtures and devices now available for home lighting.

Once you've worked out your furniture arrangement and know what you want hung on the walls, you're ready to "think theatrical" and pro-duce your lighting effects. For the family room, as for other multi-activity rooms, you'll want to plan for good overall lighting that casts glare-free light on major floor areas and traffic paths. You'll also want to include supplemental lighting for special activities, such as a spotlight for reading or downlights for playing games. In addition, you may want to illuminate artwork, show off display shelves, create a focal point, define a space, or bathe an entire wall in a soft glow to make the room seem larger.

Your choice of lighting will depend on the architecture and decor of the room, as well as on the number of purposes the room serves. The ideas on these two pages feature some of the most popular lighting effects. For details on lighting a desk or reading area, see pages 66 and 67.

Track lights for reading, wall hangings, plant, game table.

Put lighting effects on the right track

You can brighten an entire room or spotlight an activity area or piece of art with track lighting. The flexibility of track systems, teamed with the versatility of a dimmer switch, is especially helpful in a multipurpose family room. Track lights can simplify things by eliminating the need for individual table or floor lamps.

The most flexible track system has a continuous open channel. Fixtures snap into the track and swivel to send beams of light wherever you want them.

Highlight a picture

If the focal point in your family room is a picture, it deserves special lighting. The simplest, least expensive way to illuminate graphic art is to mount a picture light on the frame or on the wall behind the frame. Another, more subtle approach is to install recessed, ceiling-mounted, or track-mounted fixtures and aim them at the picture. A projector frame, unlike a spotlight or cylinder reflector, places light precisely on the picture. Best aiming angle is 30° from the vertical. Place the light too close to the wall and it will cast shadows on the picture; place it too far from the wall and the light will reflect off the picture and possibly shine in the eyes of someone sitting near the wall.

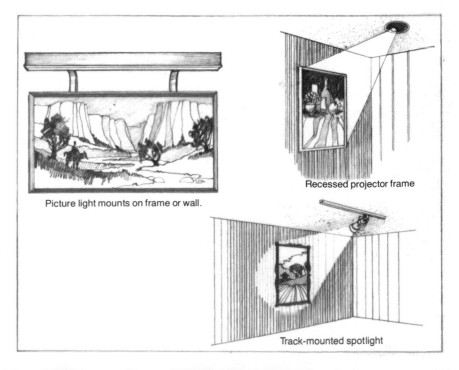
Picture light mounts on frame or wall.

Recessed projector frame

Track-mounted spotlight

Wash a wall with light

Smoothly lighting a wall—it's called wall washing—draws attention to the boundaries of the room, creating an expansive effect. You can use wall washers to focus attention on a series of pictures, highlight storage systems, enhance draperies, or dramatize a wall sculpture. The least expensive and most flexible wall washers are mounted on a track. The farther from the wall you place the fixtures, the more subdued the texture of the wall becomes and the more even the overall lighting. Conversely, lights mounted close to the wall can highlight interesting textures.

Cylinders mounted in ceiling

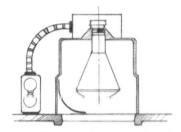

Recessed fixture needs space above ceiling. Reflector sends beam to wall.

Scoop-shaped, adjustable wall washers on track

Define areas with downlights

A type of spotlight, downlights do exactly what their name says—they send beams of light straight down. Width of the beam varies with the fixture and with the distance between the light source and the receiving surface. You can choose fully recessed, semirecessed, or ceiling-mounted downlights. Select a narrow-beamed downlight for dramatic accent over a plant or table. Or define an activity area with a medium-beamed downlight.

Downlights in deep reflector cone send narrow beams.

Downlights in reflector flood lamp send medium beams.

Bring light into display shelves

Adding mini-tracks inside shelving turns an ordinary storage/display system into an exciting piece of furniture. There's a mini-track unit that comes with a cord and plug; all you need is a screwdriver to install it. To light bookshelves, select an incandescent strip and fit it into the track. For art objects, fit the track with small spotlights. Mount a fluorescent tube on the track to help plants grow.

Incandescent strip for books

Fluorescent strip for plants

Spotlights on track for art objects

Family sunrooms

A garden view, plenty of light, and an indoor-outdoor feeling add up to the family sunroom. The rooms on these pages catch sunbeams in two different ways—by converting patios and by adding on. Either way, the indoor-outdoor atmosphere relies on abundant use of windows or sliding glass doors.

Shown on this page are two "between" rooms—family rooms made from patio space between the house and the garage. The owners had to pour new foundations for their additions, then fill in with windows and sliding glass doors to let in the sunlight.

On the next page, you'll see two other kinds of sunrooms—a patio enclosed by French doors for an airy music alcove, and an energy-saving solar addition.

When planning your own porch or patio conversion, remember that the foundation may not be up to code; if you have to lay down a new one, the conversion may be as complicated as adding a new room. Installing insulation will help the room stay cool in summer and warm in winter. Heating ducts may be extended from the house for additional comfort. A fireplace—built-in or freestanding — or a woodburning stove can also provide warmth, as well as a cozy ambience. And don't forget to plan for additional lighting.

Once a breezeway

This screened-in breezeway between house and garage is now an appealing family room. It's built partly on the old patio foundation and partly on newly laid foundation. The architect called for four sets of sliding glass doors at the sides and rear of the room and designed an open ceiling with exposed beams to retain the sun-filled, patio feeling. Track lights mounted on the crossbeams supplement the natural light. Brick-patterned vinyl makes an easy-to-clean floor covering and adds to the outdoor look of the room.
Architect: John Houk.

Garage

Recycled walls

High rafters span another former patio located between the house and garage. The old patio was torn out and a new foundation was raised level with the house floor. Wall-to-wall carpeting covers the new floor.

A sliding glass door that opens to the garden used to be the door to the patio. The contractor also recycled the exterior siding from the house and garage walls that faced the old patio, using the siding on the new exterior wall. Simple furnishings and plenty of plants complete this gardenlike family room.
Architect: Jerry Bailey.

Garage

Music and sunlight

Enclosing the patio and removing a wall created a sunlit alcove that brings music to the heart of this household. An elegant brass railing divides the new room from the dining area and marks the former outside wall. French doors that once opened onto the patio now lead to the garden and pool. Decorated in vibrant reds, the new family room is sophisticated, but still has an indoor-outdoor atmosphere—thanks to the windows, brick floor, and casual furnishings. Strategically placed spotlights illuminate the seating areas and the piano. Design: Binkley Fidge.

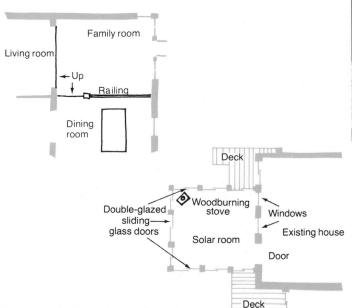

Solar roof captures sunlight

Aluminum panels along slope of ceiling snatch lower angles of winter sun for daytime warmth; woodburning stove provides heat at night. No need, then, to extend heating system of existing house to this new family room. Former exterior brick wall, windows, and door now open to cheerful, sun-filled room. Owners enjoy garden view through double-glazed, sliding glass doors. Design: Johnson Olney Associates.

Once just a garage, now a family lodge

Sometimes just one family room won't do. The owners of the family lodge pictured on these two pages wanted a family room to accommodate the frequent visits of their many relatives — not to mention stopovers by innumerable friends. When it became clear that space available inside the house would be too small, the architect turned the owners' attention to the garage.

Adding rooms above and to the back of the double garage created a large play area with windows facing the sea, a smaller area with a wood-burning stove, a spacious sleeping loft with storage, and a bathroom and dressing room.

In short, it's a children's paradise. Kids can ride a carousel horse, sneak mouth-bursting numbers of gum balls from a machine, or pull out the sliding storage drawers from under the window seats and rummage for favorite toys. Best of all, they can race up the stairway and slide down the firepole.

To build the lodge, the architect called for piers to be sunk on four corners, with a fifth pier supporting the center of the lodge. You guessed it — the fifth pier doubles as the firepole. It's a case of architectural double-entendre, proving that structural requirements can be met successfully with great wit.

Architect: Edward Carson Beall.

Room to sleep or play
A visual foil for the woodburning stove, the bricks satisfy the code requiring noncombustible material underneath and behind such an installation. Toys are stored in drawers beneath the window seat in this combination sleeping area and playroom.

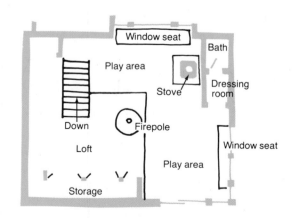

Firepole safety feature
Carpeted to match the rest of the loft, a circle of plywood covers the opening around the firepole.

Just in time for Christmas

Decked with pine and poinsettias, the family lodge designed to hold dozens of relatives and friends awaits its first celebration.

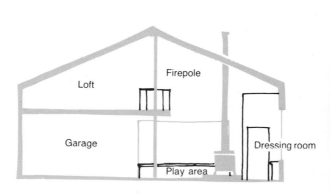

Loft

Firepole

Garage

Play area

Dressing room

Bathroom carries out mood of lodge

Like the rest of the lodge, the bathroom and dressing room are paneled with random-plank plywood. The red tub is a modern version of the classic clawfoot bath.

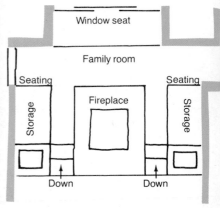

Window seat

Family room

Seating | Seating

Storage | Fireplace | Storage

Down | Down

Indoor campfire

The family and friends can gather on all sides of this square, suspended fireplace. Track lights, as well as stationary spotlights for reading, illuminate the informal indoor campfire alcove. The built-in seating has storage drawers underneath. Notice how the strong, unbroken horizontal line of the window, shades, and window seat makes the room seem wider than it is. The warm brown rug, brown tiles around the hearth, and earth-tone upholstery carry out the friendly, casual feeling of the ranch-style house and wood paneling. Architect: Samuel Romerstein.

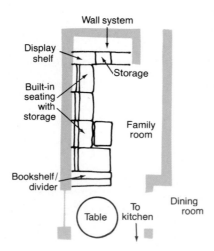

Wall system

Display shelf

Storage

Built-in seating with storage

Family room

Bookshelf/ divider

Table | To kitchen | Dining room

Look at the ceiling

Like a delicate trellis, the vent-wood ceiling hangs from the original ceiling and hides the recessed lighting above this postage-stamp-size family room. With help from hanging plants and a bookcase, it distinguishes the seating and eating areas. A ledge at the base of the wall unit opens up for magazine storage. The seats also lift up for more storage space. Earth tones in the burlap wallpaper, upholstery, and carpeting create a warm background for casual relaxation. Architects: Pennington & Pennington.

Small & cozy family rooms

You don't need a mini-barn to create a family room. A small room—carefully planned—can be a snug gathering place for family and friends.

It's a challenge to design the interior of a small room so it doesn't look crowded and stuffy like a Victorian parlor. A small room gives few options for storage and furniture arrangement, but there are ways to create the illusion of spaciousness.

Windows can do much to open up a room. Make the most of a window, especially if it provides a view. The seating area can face the window so the room doesn't turn in on itself. If it's possible to add windows, consider floor-to-ceiling vertical ones to make the room seem taller, or an unbroken line of horizontal windows to make it seem wider. A greenhouse-type window or bay window can ex- tend a room and give you space for a window seat. If you can't add windows, remember that mirrors, too, can increase the sense of space.

Furniture in a small area probably will have to be arranged along the walls, but try to avoid the waiting-room look by planning several small, intimate seating areas instead of a continuous row of chairs. The size of the furniture should be scaled to the room. A massive overstuffed couch can dwarf a small area. Built-in seating can be effective, especially with under-cushion storage.

Color should be selected with care. The more contrasting, bright colors or busy prints you use on the walls or for upholstery, the smaller and more cluttered the room will seem. Lighter colors make a room seem larger; darker colors make the walls close in.

A focal point is just as important in a small room as in a large room. If there's no natural focal point such as a fireplace or a window with a view, a floor-to-ceiling storage system can be a good substitute. Vary the shelving so you have space for art objects or collectibles, as well as books, stereo components, and possibly the TV. The wall unit should complement the architecture and the general decor without overpowering the room.

Hammock and cushions
This 10-foot-square family lounging area seems larger, thanks to its unconventional, minimal furnishings and tall windows. The half-moon shape of the wall-mounted hammock echoes the full-moon shape of the tapestry above the freestanding fireplace, drawing the eye to the room's focal point—the chimney wall. Architect: Donald Roark.

Playrooms for Adults & Kids

New pizzazz for the old rec room

If the words "rec room" make you think of table tennis in a bare basement, then you're ready for some fresh ideas from the playrooms on the next pages. Just a glance at the spunky decor and innovative design of these rec rooms will convince you that basements don't have to be bare and table tennis isn't the only game to play.

From game rooms to home gymnasiums and party rooms, here are playrooms for wherever you want them—integrated with the main-floor living areas, or under the house for the time-honored basement conversion. You'll also see specialized recreation areas, such as a video room and children's playrooms.

Rec rooms have multiple uses. The number of activities you can fit into a playroom depends on its size and your ingenuity. The larger the space, the more vigorous the games and indoor sports you can include, and the more activity areas it can handle. Yet even modest-sized rec rooms can serve many purposes if you keep storage plentiful and furniture minimal and movable. Pool tables are usually too heavy to move, but table tennis sets now come in collapsible versions. And fold-up tables and chairs can make way for indoor badminton or indoor horseshoes.

Gymnastic and exercise equipment is finding its way into more homes now that physical fitness is a way of life for many families. Some pieces of equipment, such as small balance beams, slant boards, and stationary bicycles, can be moved to the side of a rec room when the space is needed for other events. Heavy equipment, such as a barbell rack or wall pulley, will

need a permanent place but can still share recreation space.

A playroom often doubles as a party room. It's hard to give a dull party in a room equipped with amusements like pool, pinball, and darts. And if refreshments and snacks are handy at a bar, your party is sure to be a success. But be sure to check your local regulations before planning what amounts to a second kitchen: a recreation room bar and sink usually are permitted in a single-family house, but some zoning ordinances prohibit adding cooking facilities.

Custom touches in flooring, wall, and ceiling treatments can be as sophisticated or zany as you like in a playroom. You can lay down different colors of vinyl tiles or carpet tiles to make your own patterns, or continue sheet vinyl or carpeting up the wall. If you're handy with a paint brush, you can stencil super graphics on a wall or draw murals. Whatever custom finishing touches you add, the amount of wear and tear they'll have to endure should guide your materials selection.

Lively game in a lively room

Cheery red plaid rug adds the custom touch that brings this daylight basement to life. White ceiling and hearth make the small playroom seem larger and lighter. Red banquette provides spectator seating, while wicker chairs form separate conversation/reading area. Feathery greenery contrasts effectively with the bold decor. Architects: Oakmann and Stockwell.

A good setting for a party

That's what the owners wanted when they remodeled their basement. Bar to the right is a step higher than the lounge and entertainment area. Low storage unit acts as divider and pass-through. Warm wood tones, richly tiled fireplace, and special lighting in the arches above the wall beams create a relaxing scene for entertaining. Architect: Ted Granger.

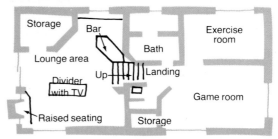

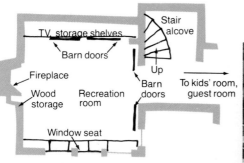

Barn doors in the basement

One set of sliding barn doors can close off this party room and sitting area from the kids' playroom. Another pair can cover the shelving in the storage wall. The rich wood of the doors and the ceiling beams sets a sophisticated "country" tone for the room. Note contrasting textures of baskets, jute-type carpet, fluffy area rug, and wicker couch. Architect: Gary Sortun.

Three super basements

Nothing drab about these basements! All three are daylight basements that divide their space into separate activity areas. The basement at the top of the facing page uses low dividers and different floor levels to distinguish the lounge and entertainment area shown from the bar, game room, and exercise area. On the lower half of the facing page, sliding barn doors divide the lounge and entertainment room from the kids' playroom. On this page, a freestanding storage unit separates a game area from the TV and storage room.

Ceiling treatments in all three basements set them apart from the ordinary and completely camouflage any "basement" look. On the upper half of the facing page, soffits frame the room and create arches for recessed spotlights above the wall beams. In the photograph below it, wooden beams match the barn doors; spotlights recessed in the white ceiling show off the storage wall. The ceiling lights in the basement on this page are just bare bulbs—but plywood, cutout stars mounted on a frame surrounding a super-graphic star give the ceiling a snazzy look, matching the decor.

Floor treatments are special, too. Textured carpeting and parquet flooring define the bar and lounge areas in the basement at the top of the facing page. Woven jute type carpeting makes an attractive — and sturdy — floor covering for the other basement on that page.

All three basements are excellent illustrations of well-planned space and decorating ideas that express the total look the owners desired.

Stellar super graphics

A big star on the ceiling and small cutout stars that hold light bulbs are just the beginning of the playful decor of this basement. There's a large circle painted on the 6-foot-tall freestanding storage unit that divides the room in half and an arched cutout frames a blackboard. Architect. Don Merkt.

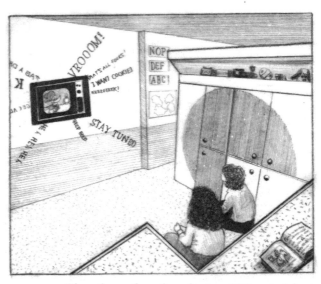

Bleachers for sleeping or TV watching

On the other side of the storage box, carpeted bleachers are roomy enough for overnight guests, reading, or TV watching. Painted words seem to radiate from the recessed TV. Architect: Don Merkt.

Sounding great! Stereo placement tips

No matter what kind of stereo you have, the final component is the room in which you place the speakers. The more soft, sound-absorbing surfaces in a room — plush wall-to-wall carpeting, overstuffed furniture, heavy draperies — the deader the sound you'll get. The more hard, sound-reflecting surfaces in a room — hardwood floors, tile, bare windows — the livelier the sound.

Place speakers in the spots you think are the liveliest, so the sound waves reach listeners with the most clarity. If you place speakers in dead areas, the high sounds may be swallowed up before they reach the listener. The speaker placement tips shown here are general guidelines for rooms with an average balance of soft and hard surfaces.

Even a speaker perfectly placed in an acoustically excellent room may seem to produce a distracting hum. The sound may actually be coming from the wires leading from the turntable into the amplifier. Using coaxial cable (insulated cable) will minimize the hum. If humming persists, check to see that AC wires aren't overlapping. If these wires must cross to complete turntable-to-amplifier hookup, cross them at right angles to stop static hum.

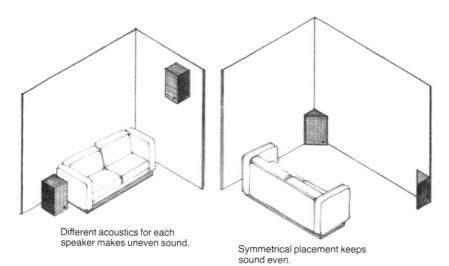

Different acoustics for each speaker makes uneven sound.

Symmetrical placement keeps sound even.

Symmetry for speaker placement

To insure even sound, speakers should be in identical acoustical situations, equidistant from the listener. For instance, if you place one speaker in a corner, put the other in the adjacent corner, not along a wall or out in the room. Likewise, if one speaker is high up on a wall, the other shouldn't be down low near a couch.

Speaker distance

The distance between speakers depends on their strength, the size of the room, and the listening positions. The weaker the speakers, the smaller the room, or the closer you sit to the speakers, the closer together the speakers should be.

The stronger the speakers, the larger the room, or the farther away you sit from the speakers, the farther apart they can be. Your goal is to achieve a balanced sound from the speakers.

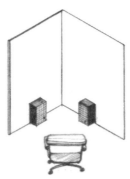

Speakers placed close together in small listening area.

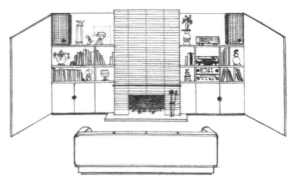

Speakers placed apart in large listening area.

Modifying the bass

You can maximize or minimize bass sounds by placing speakers in one of three positions: in the corners of a room for heavy bass sounds, along a wall for medium bass sounds, or out in the room for minimal bass sounds.

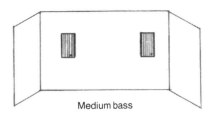

Medium bass

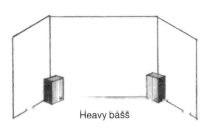

Heavy bass

Soft bass

Wall-mounted speaker

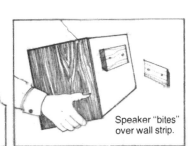

Speaker "bites" over wall strip.

Heavy-duty hanger for speakers

Hanging heavy speakers at ear level on a gypsum wall takes some ingenuity. One solution is to make super-strong hanging brackets by sawing 3/4-inch plywood down the center at a 45° angle. Use 1-1/2-inch screws to fix one strip to the speaker. Mount the other strip into the wall studs with 3-inch screws. When mounting speakers vertically, add a second spacer block of plywood to keep speakers parallel with wall. Design: Rich Edwards.

Partially recessed box of ¾" plywood holds tape deck, amplifier, records, slide-out turntable. Design: Corky Fowler and Neil M. Wright.

Component placement

Before you build or buy a cabinet or rack for stereo components, remember that:

• Components should be placed to be easily accessible. If they're too high or too low, they're hard to clean and adjust.

• Components should have good air circulation so they won't overheat and wear out too fast.

• Cabinet or rack should rest solidly on floor or wall so it acts as a sturdy foundation for the components. Shock-mount the turntable on the foundation so the needle won't skip when someone walks by or when people are dancing.

Just for kids

If kids can make believe a throw rug is a raft and a card table draped with a sheet is a monster's cave, think of what wonderful games they could invent in a play loft or attic niche!

A play area for children doesn't need to be large or elaborate to spark youthful imaginations. In fact, an odd-shaped corner in a small room may attract kids more than a large, open area with no nooks and crannies. If you're looking around for an extra playroom, consider such areas as the landing at the top of the stairs, attic space that's too short for adults, or a loft that is kid-sized.

Furnishings should be minimal. Kids use furniture differently than adults: a table becomes a diving platform, chairs are train cars, and a couch is a trampoline. Whatever you place in their play area is subject to the wear and tear they give any toy. The floor is their most popular piece of furniture, so make sure the floor covering is comfortable and easy to clean—they'll be spending most of their play time at floor level.

If you include tables and chairs in the play area, they should be kid-sized and sturdy. Avoid any with sharp corners and keep the furnishings to the side of the main romping arena so the kids won't crash into them. The bean bag chair is popular for play areas because it fits all ages, it's sturdy, and the kids have a hard time injuring themselves with it.

Toy storage is important—after all, the point of having a play area is to keep the toys and children corralled in one place, not all over the house. The more convenient and attractive the storage, the more likely the kids will pick up their toys—but we make no guarantees. Here are some storage ideas to keep the toys off the floor:

A toy closet with low, adjustable shelves labeled with each child's name may lessen quarrels about who hid the dump truck and whose puzzle that is.

Bins or toy boxes that can be rolled to the play site are easy for kids to use.

Heavy cardboard boxes, painted or papered with bright colors, make practical toy boxes. Replace them with new containers when they get bedraggled. Let the kids help decorate them.

Wooden storage boxes or fiber drums set on casters can be rolled to the site of the worst mess, quickly loaded up, and pushed out of the way.

Open shelves are good for special toys and games that shouldn't be pitched into a toy box. Modular blocks make versatile open storage.

Store ongoing games on slide-out trays or shallow drawers fitted into a cabinet. Another storage solution for unfinished games is to hinge a box-shaped lid to a table. When the lid is placed over the game, it serves as another play surface.

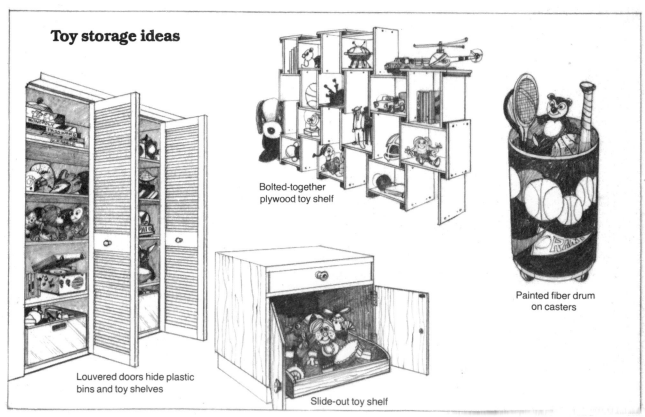

Toy storage ideas

Bolted-together plywood toy shelf

Painted fiber drum on casters

Louvered doors hide plastic bins and toy shelves

Slide-out toy shelf

An attic slide

A less imaginative design would have assigned storage to this odd-shaped attic area. Instead, carpeting the sloping floor and painting a rainbow on the wall gave the kids a jolly play area. They use resilient flooring samples to slide down what once was the roof line of the house before a second story was added. Architect: George Cody.

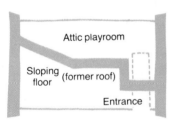

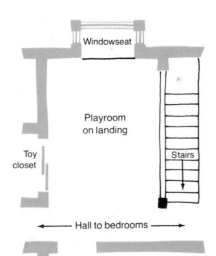

At the top of the stairs

There's room for puppets, plants, and kids on this landing. The play area has a wide window seat carpeted to match the floor; it can double as a guest bed. A storage closet to the left holds games, dolls, and a large cast of puppets. Architects: Churchill - Zlatunich - Lorimer.

Come on over & let's play...

Old-fashioned games of chance and 20th-century electronics both have a place in today's recreation rooms. But that place requires careful planning —after all, pool tables can weigh up to a ton and video tape equipment is large.

For pool, you must allow 4-1/2 to 5 feet of cuing room around the table. A pendant light or downlights are excellent choices to light the table. You'll probably want to install a cue rack and score-keeping device. Seating for spectators is another consideration.

For video tape machine, you'll need sufficient space for the oversized screen, and a place to position the projector and cassette.

For any type of recreation room, casual, comfortable furnishings and light-hearted decor help to create a playful atmosphere.

Play your favorite music
Silver-colored, laminated-plastic sheet with holes cut in it frames recessed stereo, tape systems. Cords, plugs, inner workings are hidden but accessible through storeroom in back of cedar-paneled wall. Owner can enlarge holes in plastic sheet to accommodate larger equipment, or use plastic strips to fill in around smaller replacement pieces. Architect: Ron Yeo.

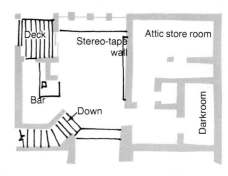

Play pool, roulette, pinball
Or try your luck at the slot machine. Designed especially for the owner's antique game tables, this L-shaped room features clerestory windows above the pool table, a bar pass-through with storage for party gear, and a plush rust-colored carpet. Adding to the casino theme of the room: a modern chandelier that looks like a gas light, and a stained-glass rendering of the tarot card of Fortune (to right of roulette wheel). Architects: Moyer Associates.

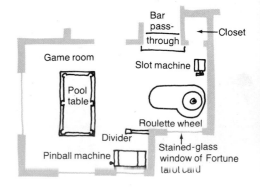

Cue up for pool

Or enjoy refreshments at the counter. This game room is a busy, open place for easy-going entertaining or everyday family fun. Skylight, recessed lights, and stained glass pendant illuminate the game area. Sunny yellow color used throughout lends more good cheer. Architect: Paul Zimmerman.

Replay a TV show

Two teenagers and their friends love to replay sports events on the big screen. And the whole family enjoys the movie theater atmosphere of the video room. Traffic flows easily from here to the game room visible to the left. Architect: Paul Zimmerman.

Fitness—a family affair

Part of a new addition, the home gymnasium doubles as a party room when balance beam and multipurpose exerciser are pushed to one side. Ceiling trusses and floodlights lend a professional atmosphere. Skylights are whitewashed in summer so room stays cool. Doors at rear lead to storage closet and spa. Architects: Prodis Associates, Inc.

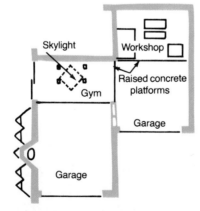

"I can do everything you can do in a gym without moving more than three feet in any direction."

That's the claim of the owner of this mini-gym. Located at the rear of a double garage (you can see the open garage door and storage wall reflected in the mirror), the mini-gym is a 7-1/2 by 11-foot raised concrete platform with heavy-duty carpet glued on it. A bolted-in-place isometric rack lets the owner place weights at different heights for various exercises. Doorway at right leads to workshop (see page 93). Architect: R. Gary Allen.

Keeping fit at home

The schools of thought on exercise — what kind and how much — are probably as numerous as the pieces of equipment in a gym. Some people pedal furiously on stationary bicycles; others prefer running, jogging, judo, or working out with weights, still others advocate a well-rounded activity program combining a number of exercises. If indoor exercise is your preference, there are ways to make room for it at home.

You can add gym equipment to an existing recreation room or create a special room for exercise. The type of equipment you include will depend on the kind of fitness program you follow. Exercise mats may be all you need. On the other hand, you may want all the gear found in a professional gymnasium: barbells, pressing station, wall pulley, slant board, punching bag, rowing machine, stationary bicycle, parallel bars, balance beam, and so forth. And if you'd like a home spa or sauna in your exercise area, you'll find the *Sunset* book *Hot Tubs, Spas & Home Saunas* full of useful ideas.

Exercise equipment comes in a wide range of

Chin-up! One ... two ... three ...
Chin-up bar fits neatly in alcove. After finishing a respectable number of chin-ups, you can catch your breath on the built-in seat.

prices. In general, the sturdier, professional quality equipment has the higher price tag. Do some comparison shopping before buying: look up "Gymnasium Equipment" in the Yellow Pages, pay several companies a visit, and try out their lines of equipment. Fitness centers, health clubs, and professional gymnasiums are good sources of equipment information, too.

For your home gymnasium

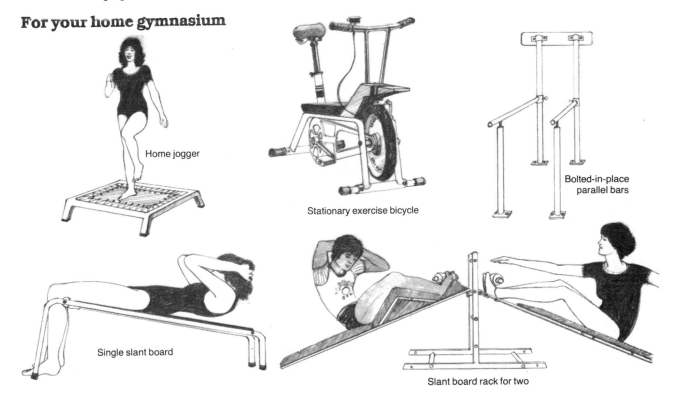

Home jogger

Stationary exercise bicycle

Bolted-in-place parallel bars

Single slant board

Slant board rack for two

For wine collectors

Candlelight flickers while good friends raise their wine glasses to sample a rare vintage—it's a wine-tasting party in your own well-stocked wine cellar! If you don't have a cool room large enough for both storage and parties, plan to do your entertaining in another area rather than sacrifice storage.

A basement isn't the only place for wine storage. Consider using the crawl space, a cool corner, or even a closet with artificial cooling. Regardless of the size of your collection or the location of the "cellar," there are four factors for successful wine storage: temperature, peace and quiet, bottle position, and light.

Temperature is best kept between 50° and 60°F (10° and 16°C), with experts generally settling on 58° (14°C) as the ideal. Controlling fluctuating temperatures is crucial: though wine can tolerate some slow temperature changes over a period of days, rapid changes will damage it.

Since temperature changes occur more slowly in the earth than in the air, many wine rooms are built near or below ground level. If you don't have a basement, consider wine storage in a consistently cool, likely storage spot. Buy several accurate thermometers and take readings over a couple of days in potential storage sites. Take the year-round temperature into consideration, as well as the proximity of heating ducts or hot-water pipes.

Insulation also controls temperature — the more you have, the better. Good insulation and a solid-core door with double weather-stripping may eliminate the need for air conditioning. But if you do decide to hook up to artificial cooling, consult an expert to obtain the most energy-efficient system.

Peace and quiet are what the wine likes. A secure rack will help, and it should be located away from sources of vibrations, such as clothes washers, dish washers, heating and cooling systems.

On its side is the correct storage position for a bottle. That way, the cork is kept wet to prevent airborne organisms from spoiling the wine. Traditionally, bottles lie in racks with corks facing out so you can get a good grip on the bottle necks. Some cellar owners string small ID tags around the necks. Others label each position in the rack. Whatever your retrieval system, you'll want to keep a log of all your wines and their locations.

Sunlight and other sources of ultraviolet light harm wine because they affect the yeast organisms still alive in the bottle. Make your wine room light-tight, but include good artificial lighting so you can tell the Riesling from the Rhine.

Unfinished basement becomes wine cellar
Take an unfinished 10 by 12 basement, line it with 3-1/2 inch insulation, install storage bins, panel the room in redwood, and you have a good start on building this wine cellar. For decor, wrap posts and beams with redwood 1 by 6s, add decorative corner brackets, and encircle one beam with a round table for wine tasting. On the ceiling, pine lath laid diagonally across tar paper creates a vineyard trellis effect.
Architect: Syd Dunton.

Half-round molding separates bottles on display shelf.

Closet "cellar"

A closet is for hanging coats, right? Not always. Here's a 38-inch-wide, 26-inch-deep closet that's an insulated, artificially cooled "cellar." Refrigerant lines and the heavily insulated walls and door keep the wine collection at a constant 58°F. (Locating the compressor in the garage is quieter than having it indoors.)

All in all, you'll be able to store 6 cases and 336 bottles in such a closet: full cases on the floor, red wine bottles stacked two deep in the middle section, and longer white wine bottles placed one deep on top. Two special display shelves can show off your rare vintages.

The main racks are made from 3/4-inch plywood with 3/16-inch aluminum rod spacers to keep the bottles in place. An elegant touch, the door and walls are lined with vinyl suede cloth. Architect: Ira Johnson.

Closet with racks display shelves.

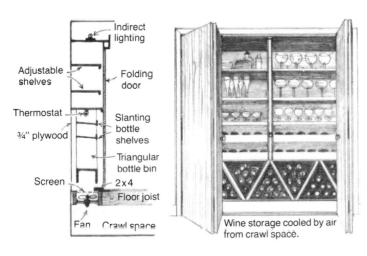

Indirect lighting

Adjustable shelves

Folding door

Thermostat

Slanting bottle shelves

¾" plywood

Triangular bottle bin

Screen

2 x 4

Floor joist

Fan   Crawl space

Wine storage cooled by air from crawl space.

Crawl-space cooled "cellar"

By taking advantage of the naturally cool air in the crawl space beneath the floor, you can construct a wine "cellar" in a storage cabinet. Two small fans under the bottle bins draw air from the crawl space through the storage cabinet and out through holes drilled in the top. A thermostat located above the top wine shelf turns on the fans to maintain an even temperature. Subfloor air stays cool enough to act as air conditioning except during very hot weather.

Triangular bins hold wines for later use. Those ready for the table are displayed in two slightly slanted shelves. Warmer upper shelves can be used for other storage. The folding doors close snugly, creating a temperature-secure cabinet that's handsome enough for a dining room. Architect: Arthur Finklestein.

Wine racks ideas

Here are four wine racks, each designed to hold bottles securely on their sides to keep the corks moist. Remember: if the cork dries out, it admits airborne organisms that spoil the wine.

Red wines will steadily improve in flavor if you age them for several years, giving tannins and acids time to blend and lose harshness.

White wines and champagne improve little with aging, but retain their quality for several years when kept in properly cooled storage.

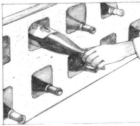

Plastered-over 8 x 8" cinder blocks provide some insulation.

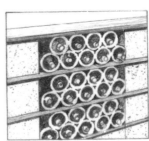

Short lengths of cardboard mailing tubes hold bottles. Concrete blocks separate board shelves.

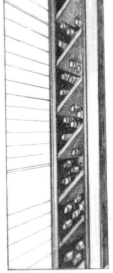

In cool garage, angled shelves built into narrow slot between garage door and wall hold wine.

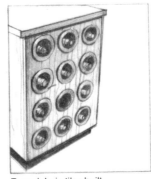

Round drain tiles built into wood cabinet hold wine snugly.

Quiet Corners

Cozy niches and retreats

Anyone who had a secret hideaway or tree house as a child instinctively recognizes the indoor, grown-up counterparts of these sanctuaries— secluded window seats, attics, and lofts. Such space, specially reserved for your private relaxation, helps you recharge your energies and view the world from a detached perspective.

On the following pages you'll see hospitable refuges that are deeply appreciated by their owners. None of the retreats is a full-fledged room that can be shut off from adjacent living areas, yet each carries out the owner's desire for a little respite from the clamor of modern life.

Sitting areas off master bedrooms, like those shown on pages 47 and 48, make excellent private areas. In both cases the owners have carefully blended the decor with the rest of the room. Notice that the sitting area on page 48 is not architecturally distinct from the rest of the suite—the furniture arrangement is all that sets it apart.

Any unused or wasted space in your house is a candidate for a quiet zone. Screens or partitions could be used to section off a corner of a room. Sliding panels and folding doors can shelter you temporarily from noise in a nearby room.

Take a hard look at your attic—it may have just enough space for a small meditation area or reading nook. Adding a loft is another possibility. Even odd angles created by the roof can be turned into retreats. Best of all, the stairs or ladders may discourage visits. Loft and attic retreats duplicate the lure of the tree house getaway, where you can be the master of your own life for a few precious minutes.

Alcoves and bay windows are also excellent candidates for retreat zones. You'll find several versions of the window seat retreat in this chapter. Some have built-in seating, others do not. Plenty of cushions and enough light for reading are the prerequisites for a comfortable window seat— a good view helps the mood, too. Adding bookshelves on either side of a window seat can create a private library nook.

Decor for retreat areas depends on your taste and on how visible the place of refuge is from other rooms. Generally, experts on color agree that red and other hot, intense colors are not as restful as blue and other cool shades.
The more contrasting colors you have in a room, the greater the sense of busyness. Juxtapose enough intense, contrasting colors and an area may look as if it's in constant motion—in short, scrambling bright colors in a small retreat corner may negate the quiet atmosphere you're trying to achieve.

Inviting retreat is part of master bedroom suite.
The lowered conversation pit retains its identity as a quiet zone though it's open to the rest of the suite. Cool blues and light wood tones give this area a Scandinavian feeling that invites you to relax and sip a cup of coffee by the fire.
Architects: Moyer Associates.

Private retreats

In an alcove, off the master bedroom, up in a loft—there are lots of places for a private retreat. Just look around your house for any unused space or odd niche, then add seating, a little light, and perhaps a small table or bookshelf.

A retreat off a master bedroom can be created by clustering furniture to make a room within a room. Using the same fabric for the upholstery and bedspread will give the room a pleasant, unified look. You can coordinate the draperies, too, if the fabric isn't overwhelming for the size of the room.

Lofts make wonderful retreats—you can literally climb above it all. If your ceiling is high enough, adding a loft to a room is rather like constructing a built-in bunk bed with only the upper bunk. If your ceiling is too low, consider removing part of it and finishing any unused attic space as a loft. Either way, you'll want to plan for adequate access. If you're very agile, a straight ladder will do. Otherwise a spiral or standard staircase is best.

A loft for snoozing or reading needn't be very large or have much headroom—think of a tiny loft as an indoor balcony. With a little planning, you may be able to slip one in a family room or living room. The space left under the loft can be used for a desk or storage.

Symphony in green and white
Two love seats, face to face, with a coffee table and a low bookcase make a room within a room. The striking green and white fabric used as upholstery, bedspread, and headboard gives the room its unified, sophisticated look. Architect: George Cody.

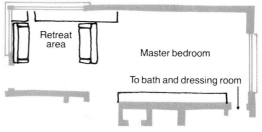

Suspended between the beams
This loft is bolted to the beams above the family room. The rhythm of the stair's handrailing continues around the loft, keeping it open and airy. The owners use the underside of the loft to display their collections of mugs and steins. To supplement its own spotlight, the loft borrows light from the family room skylight. Architect: Gary Tuchman.

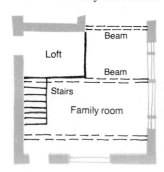

Music-listening loft

Rich colors distinguish this roomy loft. The owners asked their architect for lots of nooks and corners, so he left the end of the loft open and installed a light to make a reading niche. Besides reading, listening to music is the main activity up here. Low, casual furnishings keep the playful, relaxed feeling. Architect: George Cody.

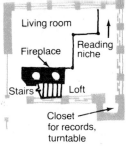

Living room
Reading niche
Fireplace
Stairs
Loft
Closet for records, turntable

Loft
Fireplace
Family room

Climb a ladder to the loft

Poised over the doorway like a miniature balcony, this loft has just enough room for one person. Because the entire area was designed to minimize the barrier between indoors and out, even the loft has windows to the garden. Architect: Charles Huff.

Sit and admire the view

Wide enough for two to lounge, this bedroom window seat takes in a spectacular view—summer sunsets are breath taking, the owners say. Upholstery on window-seat pad seems to pick up the tile pattern from the nearby suspended fireplace hearth. Seating platform has ample storage underneath. Architect: Samuel Romerstein.

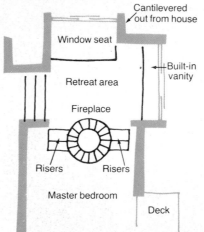

Cantilevered out from house

Window seat

Built-in vanity

Retreat area

Fireplace

Risers   Risers

Master bedroom

Deck

Stained-glass window

Entry

Built-in seat

Fireplace

Alcove

Up

Divider   Step up

Living room

Sit under a stained-glass masterpiece

Antique, stained-glass church window sheds amber glow into brick-lined alcove off living room. Cushions on curved, built-in seat leave room for fern in corner. Once a barn, house now features recycled original wood siding for weathered texture on walls, seating platform. Architect: Jim Jennings.

Five ways to sit in a window

You'll feel properly pampered when you relax in a window-seat retreat. The sun warms you and sends down excellent reading light; you'll have a pleasant view; and you'll enjoy a private niche that's separate, yet open to both indoors and outdoors.

Bay windows make superb window seats. They let in light for people and plants, and open up a view on three sides. The traditional curved bay — as well as the modern box-shaped bay — is a natural candidate for a built-in seating platform.

Small greenhouse additions are another way to create a window retreat. But, both greenhouse windows and bay windows may bring in too much sun. Direct sun may discolor upholstery, fade rugs, dry out wood floors, and make the window seat too hot. Reflective film and shades can reduce the glare; ventilation cuts down the heat build-up. Locating the window out of direct sun is the best solution.

Sit under a skylight

Small, modern bay window has a skylight above the softly padded window seat. Adjustable, track-mounted spotlight shines down from beam for nighttime use. Storage drawers underneath the seat and conveniently placed bookshelf make the area a well-furnished little retreat. Architects: Hartman-Cox.

Sit in a window box

Bookshelves on two sides and underneath the seating platform make a boxlike frame for a window retreat. Freestanding bookcases have adjustable shelves. Window seat extends into the bookcase at both ends for a built-in look.

Sit in a bubble

Intended as a dome skylight, a clear acrylic bubble makes a porthole window seat when placed in an outside wall. Dome skylights come in various sizes; a dome 4 feet in diameter is just right for a one-person window seat. Circular casing made of benderboard holds bubble in wall and forms the seat. Architect: Ray Zambrano.

Cubbyholes & hideaways

Under the stairs, behind a partition, even in a hole in the wall — cozy hideaways turn up in unexpected places.

Wherever you find the unused space for your private refuge, consider adding built-in furniture. Built-ins make better use of small odd-shaped angles and alcoves than movable furnishings. And they tend to blend, rather than obscure, strong architectural lines. Specially fitted seating platforms with storage drawers underneath and thick cushions on top work especially well in compact spaces.

If your cozy nest is to be used for reading, don't forget to plan for lighting. An adjustable, wall-mounted spotlight is a good choice. Position the fixture so the light falls from over your shoulder; otherwise it may shine in your eyes or throw shadows on your book.

As a final touch of comfort, include enough fluffy throw pillows to bolster your back or to nestle into for a snooze.

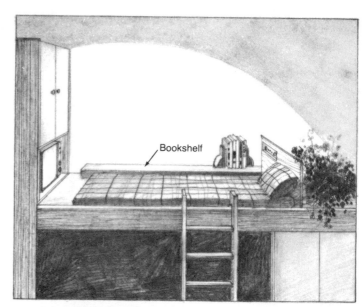

Loft nest

Perched high atop a wall, loft holds one person and one plant. You have to climb up a sturdy ladder to view the many built-in features that feather this nestlike retreat: stereo in headboard, bookshelf alongside mattress, TV and storage in wall at end of loft. Design: David Smith.

Bookshelf

Under the stairs

Often wasted space, the area under the stairs is usually too sloping to hold much furniture. But with a low, built-in platform covered with cushions and plenty of pillows, it becomes a splendid little seating area. Architect: Roderick T. Freebairn-Smith.

For people and cats

Designed as a single system, this unit provides a snug lounging niche for people and an observation platform for cats. A protruding shelf works as a table. The low storage compartment and wall-mounted boxes hold books and assorted objects. Design: The Just Plain Smith Company.

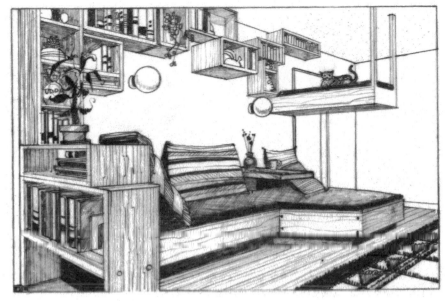

Guest nook

Where there's no natural alcove, you can use a partition to create a private corner. A standard accordion-folding door suspended from curved ceiling track is used to enclose this guest nook. The bed—a twin-size mattress on a base with storage drawers—doubles as a couch when the door is open. Design: Phoebe Common.

Nestle in for a good read

Recessed in a wall divider, this nook is equipped with a built-in bookshelf and a wall-mounted spotlight that's positioned just right for reading. Rich wood paneling inside contrasts with the white outer walls, making the niche even more inviting. Architect: Sebastian Bordonaro.

Dens, Studies & Home Offices

Comfortable spaces for desks, plenty of room for books

"What I really want for an office," confided one homeowner, "is the world's largest roll-top desk. One of those old-fashioned, Aristotelian-type affairs, with a pigeonhole for every conceivable category of office chore. Then I could let the desk systematize my work and I could roll down the top when I couldn't stand looking at it. Maybe it would do my bookkeeping for me."

We agree. A gigantic roll-top desk would make a splendid home office—especially if it could turn out paperwork for you. While you await the advent of such a prodigy, look at some of the alternatives in this chapter. A snug den might be to your taste. Or perhaps an informal library could meet your needs.

This chapter covers the spectrum from casual dens to hard-working offices. Some of the situations are complete rooms isolated from the rest of the house; others are desk areas shoehorned into closet-size places. You'll also find special sections on bookshelves, desk organization, and lighting.

The word "den" suggests a private lair where you can retreat for quiet activities. As a room, the den is a recent invention, coinciding with the decline of the formal library and the rise of more casual life styles. Most dens retain some flavor of the library or study and have a desk, as well as room for books. In addition, you'll usually find a television and a comfortable chair.

A small extra bedroom makes an easy transition to a den. Decor and furniture arrangement, rather than any special architectural features, will give the room its character. Plan to have a good reading lamp by the easy chair, task-suited lighting over the desk, and good general lighting. And don't forget display shelves for that trophy engraved "To the Best Dad in the World" and the clay cat (or is it a snowman?) your third-grader made for you.

A den, study, or home office should be protected from household noise and traffic. Just how protected you want it to be depends on the work you'll be doing and on your powers of concentration. Some people need tomblike silence and blank brick walls to get their thoughts flowing; others prefer a bit of background babble and a window with a view.

If you plan to bang away at a typewriter until dawn, you'll want to protect the rest of the household from your racket, either by distance or by sound-absorbent materials like insulation or acoustical tiles. A wall of books will help deaden sound, too.

Organization is the one aspect of any study area or home office that everyone agrees is crucial. The size of your work area influences the general layout, as does the number of activities you intend to pursue. You may want more than one work surface: one for reading and writing, and one for typing. Placed at right angles, and possibly at different levels (lower for typing), they can make an efficient work area. The general principle for organizing any study area is to arrange your equipment and supplies in the order of use. Throughout this chapter you'll find excellent ideas for efficient organization.

Just a word about home offices: Tax laws have changed recently. It is not easy to claim a home office as a tax deduction. You must use the room exclusively and regularly as a place of business for it to qualify as a possible tax deduction.

Bookshelves soar to ceiling

Part of an extensive family retreat, this library features an antique desk positioned like a command post in front of bookshelves. Besides a desk lamp, the area is lighted by a skylight and sliding glass doors; spotlights focus on art objects. See pages 86 and 87 for rest of retreat.
Architect: Sigrid Rupp.

Relax in a den

As comfortable as an old shoe, as handsome as a leather chesterfield—that's the essence of a den.

More casual than a study, more private than the family room, the den depends on decor and furnishings to create the right atmosphere. The room should cater to your comfort. Overstuffed chairs, recliners, ottomans to prop up your feet, warm pools of light reflecting off wood and leather—whatever ministers to your sense of well-being belongs in a den.

Lighting should be easy on the eyes. For good reading light, place the light source behind the reader so light comes from over the shoulder. Soft general light should be part of the scheme, too—otherwise the glare from a single reading light makes your eyes weary. If your den has display shelves or contains special wall hangings or art, use spotlights or wall washers to show them off. Strip lighting in shelves or mini-track systems in bookcases could have a place in den decor; they're unobtrusive and can add to the quiet mood.

Brown seems to be the classic color for a den, but you could be bold and decorate in whatever color relaxes you. If you decide to use the brown leather-and-wood look, consider using green plants as color accents.

All the dens shown here have the requisite mellow atmosphere. The two dens on the opposite page are tower rooms, isolated above the entire house. Your den doesn't have to be entirely cut off from the household, though quiet and privacy are important.

Cozy but sophisticated

Looking down from a loft, you see how much can be packed into a tiny area without losing the illusion of uncluttered spaciousness. Besides a fireplace, there are a stereo system, TV, storage for books, and invitingly comfortable seating. Bright throw pillows and matching chair cushion perk up the warm wood tones. Architect: Ernst Meissner.

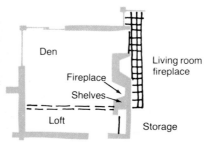

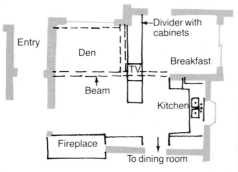

Country-casual den

Only a low divider separates the den area from the rest of the house. Plaid wallpaper on the beams carries over into the kitchen and dining room to link the three areas. The country-style furnishings proffer a casual welcome to anyone who enters the den. Design: William Kefauver.

Remote but intimate

Climb to the top of this house and you'll find yourself in a combination den and study with a spectacular view on three sides. You'll feel as though you were alone in a remote aerie, but the cozy fireplace and warm wood trim lend an intimate atmosphere. Recessed lighting in the coffered redwood ceiling adds a warm glow, while two spotlights accent the tiled hearth. Storage on either side of the fireplace holds stereo speakers, firewood, and books. Architects: Churchill-Zlatunich-Lorimer.

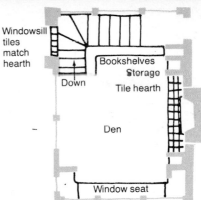

Windowsill tiles match hearth

Bookshelves

Storage

Down

Tile hearth

Den

Window seat

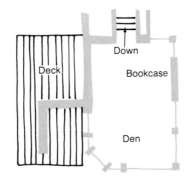

Deck

Down

Bookcase

Den

Tower den is mini-gallery

Perched on top of the house, this den contains a gallery of artifacts from around the world. You can relax on the couch, watch TV, select a book from the nearby library wall, or just contemplate the art mounted on the grass-cloth-covered wall. Strategically placed track spotlights illuminate the art objects. The tower den has access to a deck for a tree-house effect. Architects: Ellmore/Titus.

Step down to the library lounge

Centered in the sunken library, the comfy bolster-bed couch invites you to settle in for a good read. Vivid red pillows contrast with paneling, bookshelves, and ceiling beams. The couch faces a large, white wall used for projecting slides. Architect: A. Quincy Jones.

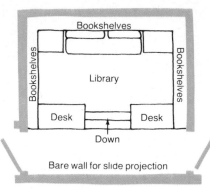

Book bridge spans room

Besides a full-height wall of books, this small combination study and guest room has a bookshelf bridge the width of the room. Attached to the ceiling joists, the bridge is sturdy enough to hold a double row of books. Architect: George Cody.

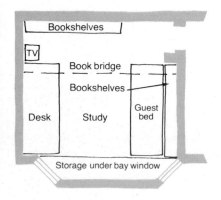

Book lover's paradise

Though the fashion for formal libraries has passed, collecting books will never go out of style. Indeed, for some people it's such a compulsion that books seem to collect themselves, multiplying until they threaten to take over the house.

For book lovers who can control their book-buying habit long enough to think about storage, these two pages contain shelving ideas for library-size collections.

Planning extensive bookshelving should take the architecture of the room into consideration. You'll notice that the bookcases shown on these pages conform to the proportions of the rooms. A bookcase, like any other storage system placed along a wall seems to become part of the structure of the room. You don't want the visual lines of the bookcase to fight with the structural lines of the room. Even if you're planning to use only a portion of a room as a library area, let the room dictate where the shelves will go.

The strong horizontal lines of a mantelpiece, molding, or windows are good guidelines for the size, shape, and position of bookcases. If the room has any unusual vertical lines or angles, try to design the shelving to complement them. If there's molding around the top of the walls, you might duplicate it around the top of a floor-to-ceiling bookcase to give the shelving a built-in look.

Built-in or attached shelving is best for a large book collection. This type of bookcase has the most stability and permanence, but the shelves themselves need not be permanent. Adjustable brackets can give them versatility. For safety and stability, wall-mounted shelves or floor-to-ceiling units should be attached to the wall studs or ceiling joists. Studs and joists can clench nails and screws firmly, but common wall-covering materials such as gypsum wallboard or lath and plaster are too soft to support heavy bookcases.

Library platform
Two steps up from the living room and you're in an open library. Building a platform is a good way to separate a library area from other parts of the room without building a wall. By being open, the library and living areas borrow space from each other. Architects: Alfred Edelman and Ivars Lazdins.

Bookcases complement wall angle
Visually part of the shape of the room, this wall of books is split by narrow windows that bring in light and relieve the massive look of the bookcase. Design: Worley K. Wong.

Build a better bookshelf

This may be your year to expand your concept of bookshelving beyond the concrete blocks and boards cherished during your student days.

The basic requirement for a bookshelf is that the shelving material and its supports be strong enough to bear the weight of your books. The thinner and less rigid the shelf material, the closer together the supports must be.

Popular shelving material includes lumber, plywood, particle board, and hardboard. To test how far a shelf will span and how much weight it will hold without bowing, support the ends with a couple of chairs and load it with the weight it will have to hold. If it bows, select a thicker material or add a support in the center. Remember, too, that some books are heavier than others. Finally, consider whether you want permanent shelves or adjustable ones, a freestanding system or shelves attached to the wall. Freestanding bookcases can double as room dividers; attached shelving systems tend to look like part of the architecture.

The bookshelves on these pages are slightly more complicated than blocks and boards. For additional ideas and how-to information, see the *Sunset* book *How to Make Bookshelves & Cabinets.*

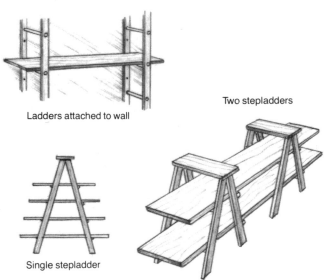

Ladders attached to wall

Two stepladders

Single stepladder

Stepladders & boards
If stacking boards on concrete blocks is the zenith of your building skills, this project is for you. For the simplest version, use two stepladders with rungs at equal heights; paint or finish the ladders as you like; place them back to back and run shelves through the rungs. Using a single ladder is slightly more complicated—you'll have to fasten cleats on the side without rungs to support the shelves. For yet another version, fasten two ladders to the wall, then run shelves through the rungs.

Bookshelves in a closet
The easiest way to have a built-in bookcase is to take over a shallow closet. Remove any shelving and shelf supports and paint or panel the closet as you choose before installing a new shelf-support system. Decide on the number of shelves you want, then paint the shelves or face them with paneling strips to match the closet. Now you're ready to select new shelf mounting —it can be blocks, bars, or brackets. For enclosed storage, use hinges to attach a door to the bottom shelf, as shown. Design: Camp Brothers Home Remodeling.

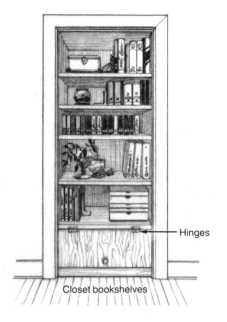

Hinges

Closet bookshelves

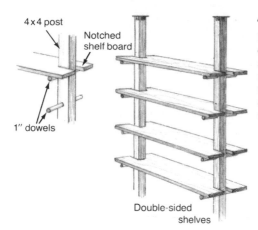

4 x 4 post

Notched shelf board

1″ dowels

Double-sided shelves

Two-faced room divider

Building this dual-purpose bookshelf requires some carpentry skill. You'll have to notch the shelving to fit around the floor-to-ceiling 4 by 4 posts, and you'll have to drill holes in the posts to receive the 1-inch dowels that support the shelves. Fasten the posts to the ceiling joists with L-brackets. Sand all edges lightly, then finish the unit as you please.

Hide the hardware

Track and bracket systems make easy-to-assemble adjustable shelving. In this version, metal tracks are screwed into 2 by 4 posts, rather than into the wall. Brackets are turned toward the wall. Posts, which extend from ceiling to floor, should be secured with adjustable furniture glides if you don't want to nail or bolt them to the ceiling joists. Because the brackets face the wall, the unit has a customized look. Painting or finishing the posts and shelving can make this simple system even more sophisticated.
Design: Stuart Goforth.

Track and brackets screwed to posts

Bookshelf hides light fixture

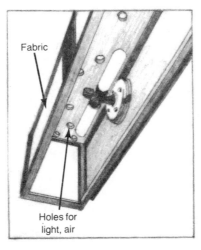

Fabric

Holes for light, air

Bookshelf with an inner glow

A pair of light fixtures hides under this shelf. Placed above a desk, it makes an attractive lamp shade and holds books at the same time. For the frame, nail together fir 1 by 1s reinforced by crosspieces along the front and top. Sand and finish the wood as you like. Drill 1-inch holes in plywood cut to fit the top (these let out light and heat). Screw the plywood to the top of the frame, then stretch and staple fabric inside the frame. Position the shelf over the light fixtures and bolt it to the wall studs. Design: Robert Griffin.

Studies that are positively professorial

Books, books, and more books, plus a hard-working desk and perhaps an easy chair—a study doesn't need much else.

If you're planning a study for your home, storage for writing supplies and books will be your main concern, along with lighting and seating.

Lighting should serve in three ways: general illumination, light for writing, and light for reading. You'll find helpful ideas on pages 66 and 67.

Of all the furniture in the study, the desk chair probably is the most important. A standard secretary's chair is a good choice because it supports your lower back while you write or type. Seats on these chairs usually are adjustable, so—no matter what your height—you can place your legs at a comfortable angle.

Chairs and work surfaces that are too high or too low can make you miserable during long work sessions. So shop around for comfortable, good-looking study furniture. At an office supply store, you'll find that much of today's business furniture is realms away from the utilitarian, gray metal designs of the past. See pages 72 and 73 for office organization tips.

Tower of books
Study is tower addition for professor with a virtual library of books. Long work tables give him plenty of room for research materials, typing, and writing. Sturdy floor-to-ceiling shelves on one wall, hold his books. Architect: George Cody.

Reference counter
End wall has sloped, waist-high counter for heavy reference books. Above-counter bookshelf has fluorescent light to help when you look up facts.
Architect: Morgan Stedman.

Double study
Partition between built-in, L-shaped desks keeps his work from hers. The two halves of the study are almost mirror images of each other. Track and bracket shelves hold books. Architect: George Cody.

Perfect for paperwork

If a highly polished study could bring forth highly polished prose, then this is the place to work. The oak-paneled study makes reading, writing, and research a pleasure. A skylight illuminates the room during the day; reading lights turn on at night. Bookcases have both cabinets and shelves for storage. Architect: Harry Rodda.

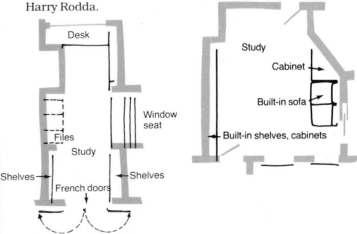

Maximum use of minimum space

Shoehorned into a long, narrow area, this study takes advantage of every possible inch of storage space. Open shelves hold books, while drawers under the bench keep papers organized. Located in a little-used passageway, the study is off the game and video rooms that appear on page 41. Architect: Paul Zimmerman.

Take a slice from the living room

And turn it into a study. The open design of the house didn't provide a private space for a study, so the architect took a narrow slice off the living room and enclosed it with a high room divider. Result: a warm, pleasant place to work that's secluded but not totally isolated. Architect: George Cody.

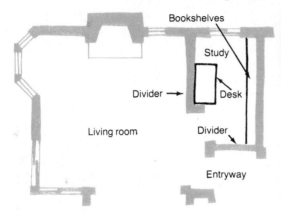

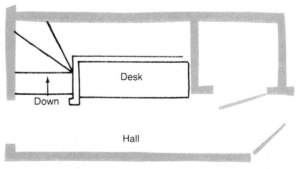

It used to be a planter box

The skylight overhead used to bring light to plants; now it brightens a work area. Desperate for a "command center" to organize her work, the owner replaced the planter box with a large table. Now she can keep track of the rest of the household from her desk in the main hallway. Suspended light supplements the skylight. Crisp-colored modern prints decorate the wall on the other side of the staircase.
Architect: Robert C. Peterson.

Tucked-away desks

You don't have to turn an entire room into an office or study to make way for a hard-working desk. Look around for an alcove or any other unused or wasted space and imagine a desk and chair there.

The desk areas on these pages seem to prove that the more unusual the space, the more imaginative the solution. One desk is tucked under the staircase, another was once a planter box. You'll see a fold-up desk that blends into a blank-faced room divider, a desk area sliced from a living room by a high wall, and a desk that wraps around a bed.

Under the stairs
Bifold door cut to match the angle of the staircase opens to reveal built-in desk and shelves. A file cabinet fits neatly into its own closet under the stair landing. Architect: George Cody. Associate: William Smart.

Hidden in a room divider
When it's closed, it's a blank-faced room divider. When it's open, you see two separate storage areas with a desk in the middle. A fluorescent strip lights the desk, supplementing the ceiling track lights. Even the chair slips into the unit when it's time to close up. There's room on the top for indoor greenery. Architects: Pennington & Pennington.

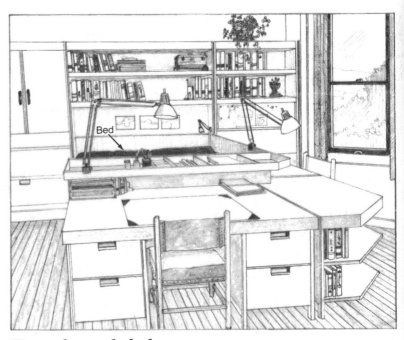

Bed

Wrapped around a bed
This wraparound desk is an imaginative solution to the problem of too little work space. The whole tidy unit breaks down into modules, so the apartment-dwelling owners can move it easily. Adjustable table lamps can be clamped on wherever light is needed. There's actually room enough for two people to sit and work here. Storage is below the desk, in pull-out file boxes and open shelves. Architect: Jennifer Clements.

Good light for reading, writing, typing

Do you squint when you read, write, or type? Your weary eyes might be suffering because of poor artificial lighting: a light shining in them instead of on your book or desk, a background light that's too dim, or a single bright task light contrasting sharply with a dark room. Or perhaps the natural light is to blame: window light on the wrong side of the work surface, shining into your eyes instead of over your shoulder.

To avoid eye strain, give some thought to the lighting around your desk or reading area. Here are some things to keep in mind:

Diffused, overall light should be glare-free background illumination. A window or skylight can provide good natural background light. Artificial background light doesn't have to be dazzling — only about a third as bright as the light that shines directly on your book or desk. You may want more than one source of artificial background light, to cast as few shadows as possible. Your choices in fixtures include ceiling-mounted fluorescent or incandescent bulbs or tubes (with or without diffuser shades) and track lights that throw a wide enough beam.

Task lighting should direct a beam of light to your desk or book without glaring in your eyes or reflecting harshly off papers or book. Clamp-on adjustable lights, standard lamps, track-mounted spotlights — indeed any light source guided by a cylinder or shield—can succeed as task lighting if you position it so it shines on your work, not in your eyes.

Task light for reading, writing, and typing shouldn't be placed too close to the desk or book or it will reflect uncomfortably off the paper. Position it to shine over your shoulder onto the work surface or book. If you're right-handed, light should come over your left shoulder so your writing hand won't cast shadows on the paper. If you're left-handed, light should come down over your right shoulder.

Reflected light is important, too. The lighter the wall and ceiling color, the more reflection you'll have. You can bounce a directed beam of light off a white wall to supplement general light. The desk shown at the top of the next page benefits from spotlights reflecting off a sloping ceiling.

Lighting ideas

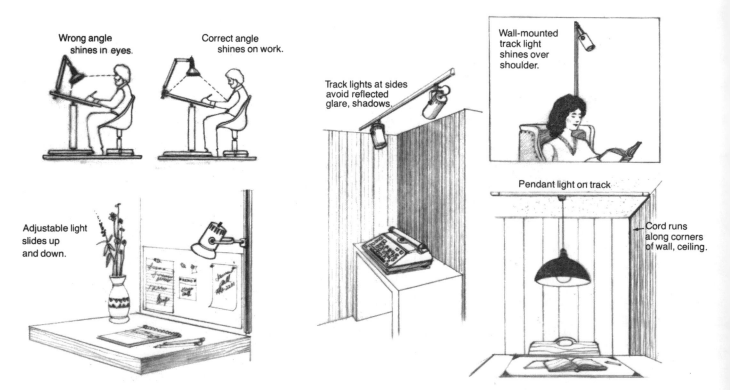

Wrong angle shines in eyes.

Correct angle shines on work.

Adjustable light slides up and down.

Track lights at sides avoid reflected glare, shadows.

Wall-mounted track light shines over shoulder.

Pendant light on track

Cord runs along corners of wall, ceiling.

Four sources of light in one study

Sloping ceiling that reflects spotlights back into the desk area is just one of the good lighting ideas in this room. Clamp-on adjustable light provides task light; window and skylight are two sources of natural light. Architect: Kathy E. Schmidt.

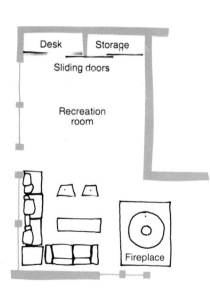

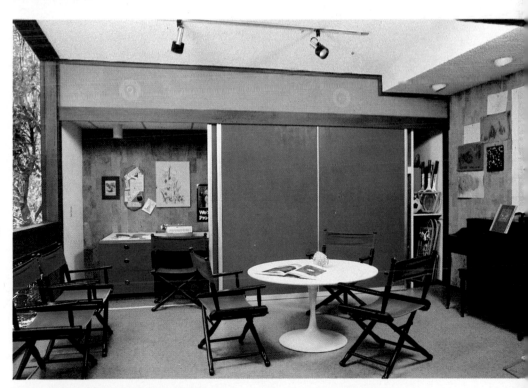

Downlight in an upbeat study

Protruding downlight illuminates the desk revealed when the sliding doors are pushed back. Track lights and a large window provide the background light in this colorful multipurpose room. Architect: Jim Jennings.

Office shares cheerful guest room

Just because it's pretty doesn't mean it's unpractical. This office-guest room was remodeled for maximum work conditions and a feeling of spaciousness. There's a drafting table that gets plenty of use. Behind it is a desk unit with slats for blueprints, open shelves for supplies, closed storage for catalogs, plus space to type and work. Cabinets are kept simple, so the room doesn't look cluttered. Pastel floral wallpaper and yellow guest-bed cover add fresh color. White ceiling and cabinetry help to make room seem larger. Architect: Jean Crawford.

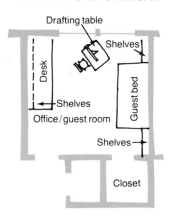

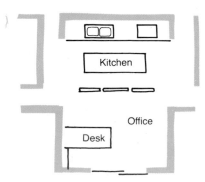

Space-sharing offices

Space sharing can happen in different ways. It occurs when a room has two or more distinct purposes — such as an office doubling as a guest room. Or two separate areas can borrow visual space from each other — such as an office loft sharing the open space around it with lower rooms.

The pretty, pastel-colored office-guest room on this page is a good example of a room doing double duty. Careful storage planning and a delicate palette of decorative colors give it a tidy, unified look.

The other three offices shown here share space by visually borrowing from other rooms. Tinted glass panels modify the shared zone in the office-kitchen area on this page, keeping the two rooms open but distinct. On the facing page, loft offices share views with the rooms below them, yet their height separates them from the lower part of the house. The gallery office on the upper half of the facing page does it all: it's a multipurpose "room," as well as a loft.

Office's "sunglasses" shade kitchen

Bronze-tinted glass panels supported by aluminum poles act like sunglasses, reducing the glare of the western sun as it shines through the office into the kitchen. The see-through panels allow both rooms to share space and light. Contemporary sculpture and furnishings enhance the modular architecture of the house. Architect: Charles Stewart.

Office gallery connects more lofts

Innovative remodeling turned a barn into this gloriously spacious home. The office gallery loft—running between additional lofts at either end of the "barn"—includes work desk, lounge area, organ, and guest bed. Windows are covered by vent-board panels, complementing the wood paneling of the gallery. Architect: A. Quincy Jones.

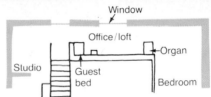

Office loft over master bedroom

Sharing a woodsy view through windows and skylight panels, the office loft extends over the master bedroom suite. Going up the stairway, you pass a wall of bookshelves, storage, and display space. Once in the loft, you can work in a quiet atmosphere without being cut off from the rest of the house. Architect: E. Paul Kelley.

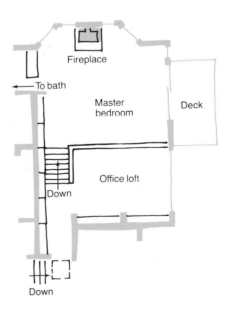

Her office is a broadcast studio

Corner desk is a compact radio station with room for typewriter and broadcast microphone. Twin canister-type lights beam down on desk area. Two built-in wall units provide three kinds of open storage shelves: regular bookshelves, slanted magazine racks, and vertical slots above the desk. Design: Peter Van Dyke.

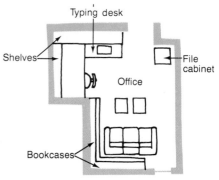

His office is a writing studio

Corkboard lines one side of this small, rectangular office; storage unit on the other side has bookshelves, magazine rack, and typing cabinet. Two filing cabinets support the walnut desk top. Typing cabinet has slide-out top for typewriter, open shelves for paper and telephone books (see page 72 for detailed drawing). Adjustable recessed lights, clamp-on desk light, and natural light provide ample illumination. Design: Peter Van Dyke and Tim Cook.

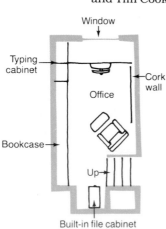

His-&-her home offices

Do working couples need double work space at home? Sometimes. The couple pictured on the facing page solved a work space problem by using two separate rooms. The owners of the offices on this page share working space.

All three offices make maximum use of space. On the facing page, "her" built-in, ceiling-high desk unit features vertical spacers that organize desk supplies, reference books, and telephone books. Bookcases in both "her" and "his" offices include slanted racks for two rows of magazines. Both desks rest on file cabinets.

On this page, both offices make use of former closet space. The two desks shown at left are in a former entryway; one is in the old coat closet, the other is next to a floor-to-ceiling storage cabinet. The his-and-her office shown below was once a study with two closets. The closets are now part of a desk and shelving system. The shelves slip between grooves formed by cedar slats lining the entire room. A cabinet that extends into the middle of the room and wide filing cabinets under a counter on the back wall provide more storage and work space.

Models of efficient planning, all these home offices show you how to make the most of available space.

Cedar-paneled double office
Rows of cedar slats—separated just enough to hold a bookshelf—give this 12 by 12-foot home office its bold horizontal pattern. Before the paneling was installed, the walls were painted black so the grooves between the slats would be distinct. A double desk counter extends across two former closets. Lighting is ample: fluorescent strips in each desk alcove, recessed indirect lighting in the soffits, and track lights that replaced the original overhead fixture. A storage cabinet divides his desk area from hers, providing additional work surface and storage. Architect: John Caldwell.

Once an entry, now a two-person office
An extensive remodeling job moved the front entrance, so the architect took advantage of the old entry space and turned it into a small home office for both husband and wife. Desk at right is in a former closet. The front door used to be straight ahead, now it's a full-length window. Architect: Duaine Duff.

Home office helpers

Better than a personal secretary or an executive assistant, well-organized storage is the most valuable home office helper you can have.

Whether you install traditional gray file cabinets or go modern with stacks of colorful plastic-covered wire bins, style isn't as important as the arrangement of your storage. Frequently used items like resource materials and writing and typing supplies should be in storage that's easily accessible. Less frequently used items can go on high, less accessible shelves, or in a supply closet out of the office area.

While built-in, custom-made storage is nice to have, you might want to investigate office and business furniture stores for bargains in new or used storage cabinets, file systems of all sizes, desk-top organizers, chalk boards, bulletin boards, partitions, lectern to hold your unabridged dictionary, and other office furnishings. Business furniture isn't as drab and institutional looking as it used to be. And used office furniture can be recycled through imaginative refinishing or a paint job.

The storage ideas shown here may be just the helpers you need to complete your home office.

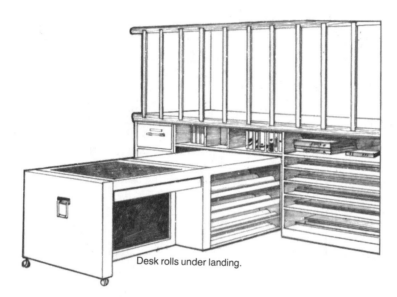

Desk rolls under landing.

Roll out the counter

A split-level house often has dead space that can be turned into office storage. In this system, a roll-out counter becomes desk-size when pushed under next level of house. Wide shelves to right of desk hold prints; typewriter, file drawers are on other side. Extended, counter provides large surface area to sort prints, storage underneath for wrapping paper. Dead space under stairs could be used in a similar manner. Architect: Robert Garland, Jr.

Organize your typing paper

Typing and writing supplies are at your finger tips in this cabinet set at right angle to main desk. Low, wide open shelves also hold telephone books. Top slides out to bring typewriter into position. This cabinet is part of a wall-storage unit (see page 70), but you might adapt the idea for a freestanding cabinet. Design: Peter Van Dyke and Tim Cook.

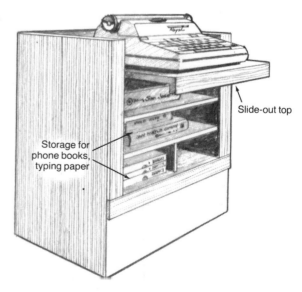

Slide-out top

Storage for phone books, typing paper

Split-level organization for desk drawers

If you've recycled old standard cabinets to hold a desk top, you can improve their efficiency by adding two-level drawer dividers. Patterned after a store-keeper's till, a 1-1/8-inch-deep sliding, lift-out tray sits on top of the lower dividers. Tray is made from pine strips glued to a plywood base. Lower dividers are 1/4-inch hardboard strips set into slots routed in the 1/2 by 2-1/2-inch pieces of pine that line the drawer. Design: Janean.

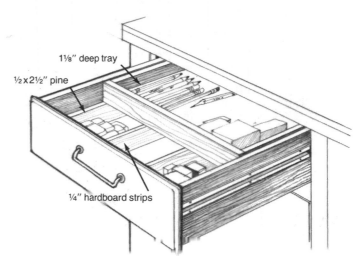

1⅛" deep tray

½ × 2½" pine

¼" hardboard strips

Desk-top book end

Organize your reference books with this sturdy book end. It will keep them handy on your desk and won't fall over the way smaller book ends do. Easily adjustable, the ends slide along the spine but bind stubbornly when books lean against them. A single 24-inch piece of 1 by 8 mahogany (or any wood) cut into three pieces as shown is all you need. Position spine on end pieces and trace around it carefully, then cut slots with a coping saw or saber saw. Spine should just barely slide through snug slots.
Design: Gary Williams

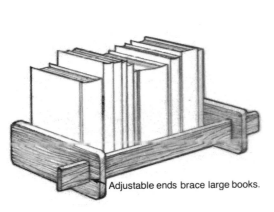

Adjustable ends brace large books.

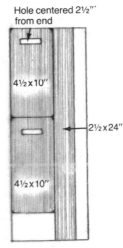

Hole centered 2½'" from end

4½ × 10"

2½ × 24"

4½ × 10"

Open file with Scandinavian look

Unvarnished dowels make a desk-top, open file for folders of work in progress, correspondence, or books. Base of rack is 3/4-inch dowels drilled to receive 3/8-inch dowels for end braces and upright dividers. Glue holds the file together.

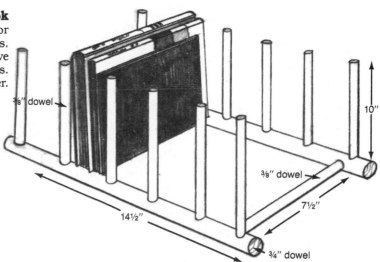

⅜" dowel

10"

⅜" dowel

7½"

14½"

¾" dowel

The Arts at Home

Studios, craft rooms, workshops, darkrooms

The creative genius within you will rejoice at the studios and workshops in this chapter. To an artist, these are dreams come true—well-equipped, well-lighted studio spaces that bring out the best of their owners' talents.

Even if your involvement with arts and crafts runs more to Halloween and Christmas decorations than to oil painting, you'll find these studios and workshops full of ideas applicable to small-scale setups.

Your studio—whether a corner in the family room or an entire converted garage—should be both comfortable and functional. A studio cluttered with paraphernalia matches the romantic notion of "Great Artist at Work": tubes of oils squeezed from the middle; floor and tables bristling with sticky brushes; canvases stacked higgledy-piggledy; ramshackle furniture and a kaleidoscope of props. More likely, such an environment houses a "Great Artist Struggling to Get Organized."

The goal of good studio planning is to tailor a space to fit your work. "Dry" crafts like weaving have specific needs that are very different from "wet" crafts like ceramics. Jewelry making can take place in a relatively confined area, but if you're painting large canvases, you'll want to be able to step back and get a perspective on your work.

Studio location also will depend on the art or craft. The less mess, noise, or smell that goes with an activity, the more likely such studio space can be integrated into a living area within your home. There's no need to exile yourself to the garage if you paint watercolor miniatures— unless the bustle of household activities bothers you. On the other hand, there are good reasons for placing a metal-sculpture studio out of the house: welding is noisy and the work area may look like an auto parts shop.

As you gaze at the studios that follow, watch for storage ideas, solutions to lighting problems, ways to organize work flow, and materials for flooring and walls. By picking out an idea here and a suggestion there, you can custom design your own studio.

"The wooden cocoon I wrap myself in"

That's the way the artist describes his delightful studio. The spacious 28 by 28-foot, open beam studio brims with ideas you could use in smaller set-ups: good northern light; track lights; furnishings arranged for maximum efficiency and comfort; supplies and materials handy in colorful storage files and cabinets. Architect: Francis Palms.

Ceramics, sculpture & weaving studios

Ceramics — a wet, potentially messy craft — and metal sculpture — a noisy, usually messy medium — contrast with the more placid art of weaving in the home studios shown on these two pages.

All four studios are well organized, with excellent storage facilities and lighting. They're located to suit the craft and their owners' work habits.

The ceramics studio below is out of the main traffic area, keeping interruptions away from the potter and mess away from the rest of the house. At right, metal sculpture and other crafts are pursued in an open structure set apart from the house, so smells and noises are out of household range. The weaving room at the bottom of the facing page is near the main living area, but in a quiet zone. The weaving studio shown above it is, as the owner wished, more isolated from the main part of the house, creating a cozy world unto itself.

Roomy, open studio for sculpture
Metal sculpture is just one of the arts practiced in this two-part studio. The stained-glass window was made here, and there is equipment for wood sculpture, as well as forging and welding. Sliding door can be closed to separate the work areas. Architect: Robert Stoecker.

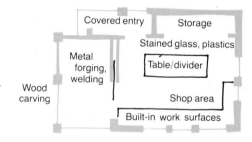

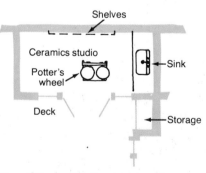

Small but efficient ceramics studio
Greenware (unfired ceramics) on wall-mounted, open shelves and glazed ceramics on freestanding shelves are clear signs that this is an efficient place to work. Opening onto a pool deck, the tidy studio is situated away from the main part of the house — another factor contributing to its high production rate. Architects: Goodwin Steinberg Associates.

Weaving studio is a world of its own

"It's mine!" cheers the owner of this loom room, as she explains that she wanted a studio that could be closed off and turned into a private craft retreat. A wood-burning stove heats the 15 by 18-foot room. Glowing wood tones of parquet floor and built-in storage system, plus well-displayed handicrafts create an inspiring atmosphere. Architect: Stephen Sontag.

Garage

Storage

Utility

Up

½-bath

Laundry

Shelves

Bath

Woodburning stove

Studio

Shelves

Old-fashioned craft in modern setting

Lyrical sweep of windows brings abundant natural light to this elegant weaving studio. Track lights supplement natural light when needed. White, light-reflecting walls show off woven arts collection, making the room as pleasant to look at as it is to work in. Architect: Phillip Schwimmer.

To living room

Desk

Studio

Storage

Garage studio with storage to spare

Plentiful open storage and roomy work surfaces make this converted garage an efficient studio for crafts and art work. Removable panels in wood frames line the ceiling, with space left for skylights. Sisal mats cover the concrete floor. Window seat, and sitting area let studio double as pleasant retreat. Architect: Sylvia Reay.

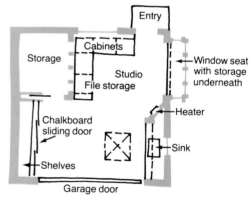

Airy, light studio for wet, messy work

By expanding his garage, the artist gained enough studio space to make his own paper. The studio has both a skylight and fluorescent lighting, plus a sink, work counter, and bathroom. Vacuum table in center of studio suctions water from paper pulp. Excess water flows through hose to drain in cement floor. Design: Rick Davidson. and Joe Zirker.

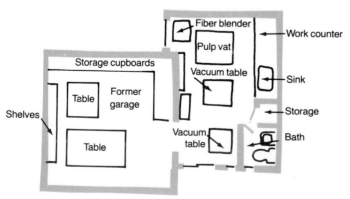

Art in the garage

A Bohemian garret may encourage an artist's creativity — but sometimes a little studio space alongside the family station wagon is all that's needed. On the facing page you'll find a garage expanded to include a studio for making paper, and a multipurpose garage studio. On this page,
one garage shares studio space with a car, another is crowned with a skylight, and a third was almost entirely rebuilt to house a painting studio.

As you eye your own garage for possible conversion, keep these factors in mind: you'll have to park the car somewhere; unless you have heavy equipment to move in and out, you'll probably want to remove the garage door and fill in its space; the garage surely will need major remodeling for natural and artificial light; it may need insulation and heating; wiring may be inadequate; the concrete floor may have a slight pitch— not to mention being uncomfortable for long periods of standing; and plumbing may have to be added if your craft requires a water supply.

If you can solve those problems—many of which call for professional help — you'll have a large, quiet work space that will be the envy of your fellow artists.

Studio shares space with cars
The minute the cars roll out, this garage can be transformed into a studio. Supplies and equipment are stored in a cabinet along one wall. Acrylic-paneled sliding doors on the rear wall let in light and breezes. Architect: Dartmond Cherk.

Greenhouse brings in light
All but two walls of the old garage came down to make way for a painting studio. The roof angles to a peak on the north side, where it abuts a prefabricated greenhouse unit. There's a variety of artificial lighting: ceiling-suspended fluorescents; pendant lighting; track-mounted floodlights; globes on the main roof beam; and an adjustable, clamp-on table lamp. Architect: Harley Jensen.

Crowning skylight
Soaring new roof on the old garage is topped with a clear plastic skylight. Shelves and work tables are suspended from the rafters. Placed in the center of the studio, potter's wheel benefits from the glorious natural light. Architect: Lawrence Steiner.

Studio storage

Your work habits and temperament are as important as your materials when it comes to planning storage in a studio. You may want to keep supplies out of sight, then select what you want and bring it to your work table. Or you may feel that if all possible materials aren't out in the open within arm's reach, they may as well be in China.

Whether you're the fastidious, keep-everything-out-of-sight type or the more casual keep-everything-within-reach type, you'll want to follow this simple principle: store frequently used supplies close to the work area and in the order

that you use them. If possible, materials and tools used together should be stored near each other.

Be sure to label storage boxes or drawers — especially for rarely used, hard-to-reach items — so you won't forget what's in them. Poisonous chemicals should be clearly labeled and kept in locked cabinets.

The way supplies are stored in a craft shop or art store can show you how to arrange your materials. While you can buy special-purpose storage units like those in an art shop, you can also construct your own shelves and systems; the *Sunset* book *How to Make Bookshelves & Cabinets* can give you some guidance. Since esthetics rarely matters in a studio, you don't need much skill to build serviceable storage. Adjustable track-and-bracket shelving is easy to install. Or you could use freestanding, industrial-type, metal units with extra-wide shelves.

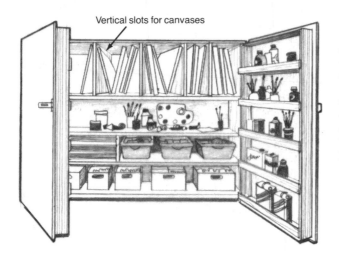

Vertical slots for canvases

Armoire for art
Shelves on the insides of its double doors increase the storage in this art pantry. Cabinet could be built-in or freestanding. In center section, top shelf has vertical slots for stretched canvases and frames; most frequently used paints and supplies are easily accessible on the middle shelf; lower shelves hold labeled containers for less-needed supplies. Padlock on doors keeps kids out. Architect: Dartmond Cherk.

Groovy duplex cabinets
Depending which way you install pregrooved plywood in a cabinet, you can have instant vertical or horizontal storage shelves. Pregrooved plywood is a type of exterior house siding with grooves already milled into it. Outdoor siding is often treated with preservative; avoid buying panels with a heavy preservative odor. In the cabinets shown, pregrooved plywood lines 2 by 3-foot frames. Right side has pregrooved plywood on top and bottom for vertical storage; left side has plywood on sides for horizontal storage. You could line an existing cabinet or build from scratch. Either way, be sure to line up the grooves precisely or the shelves won't slide in properly.

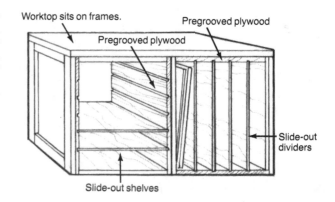

Worktop sits on frames.

Pregrooved plywood

Pregrooved plywood

Slide-out dividers

Slide-out shelves

Canvas sling shelves

You start with tracks and brackets, but instead of board shelves, sling lightweight canvas strips between brackets to make loose compartments for yarn or other light supplies. Cut each canvas strip 2 inches wider than length of brackets. For "shelf" length, just allow enough material so slings span the brackets loosely. Stitch a 1-inch hem on both sides of the strip. Starting at one end, fold and stitch down 3 inches for each loop. Slip loops over brackets.
Design: Darle Maveety.

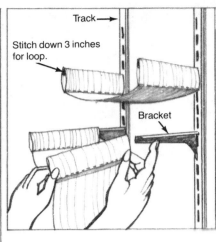

Track

Stitch down 3 inches for loop.

Bracket

Canvas slings hold light-weight supplies.

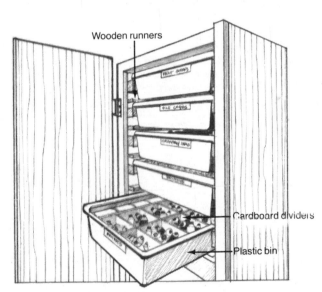

Wooden runners

Cardboard dividers

Plastic bin

Pull-out plastic drawers

Plastic bins, purchased from stores that supply offices, restaurants, or schools, make sturdy drawers for art or craft materials. You can put together a drawer-filled storage cabinet using plastic bins and small wooden runners. Nail runners to the cabinet's side walls—two runners per side—to hold the lip of each bin. Make sure the runners are nailed exactly opposite each other or the bins will be wobbly and won't pull out smoothly. The bins shown are 3-1/2 by 13-3/4 by 19 inches.
Architect: Boyd A. Blackner.

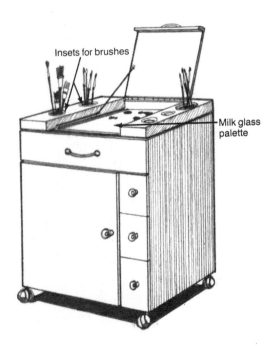

Insets for brushes

Milk glass palette

Traveling taboret

Like a miniature studio on wheels, this well-equipped taboret can be rolled to wherever the light is best for painting. Your brushes—carefully cleaned, of course—stand bristle end up in jars inset in the top. Open the hinged lid to mix colors on the milk glass palette. Paint tubes, brush cleaners, paint thinners, sketching supplies, and other materials are stored in the pull-out drawers and cupboard section. A similar design could be adapted for crafts or other art media.
Design: Phyllis and Dick Ham.

Pavilion or pullman—ways to separate art from daily life

A separate, specially designed studio — like the one shown at the top of these two pages — ensures privacy and makes it clear that the artist steps into another world when she or he takes up pencil or paints.

If an art pavilion isn't possible, a small addition with a separate entrance — like the studio shown on the lower half of these two pages — may get you far enough away from the rest of the household to pursue your art or craft in peace.

Either way, you'll probably want the architecture and exterior of the studio to complement your house.

Outside the art pavilion
A wall bridges the studio and the garage, but it's for looks only: the studio is entirely separate. Modern architecture matches main house. Studio entry is in small atrium garden between garage and pavilion. Architect: Clement Chen.

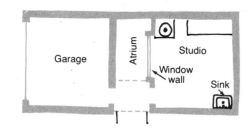

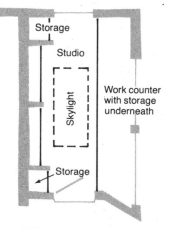

Outside the pullman studio
Only 9 feet wide, this railroad car-style studio was added alongside the garage, but has its own entrance. Wood floor placed above garage level aligns studio windows with the grade of garden and pool. That way, visual space extends into the garden so the skinny studio seems larger. Architect: David Raphael Singer.

Inside the art pavilion

Sloping upper portion of north window wall captures light for painting. There's a rack to hold paintings and a rolling taboret for supplies—both specially designed. Rug under easel makes long painting sessions easier on the feet. In the lounge area, artist can sit down and give painting a critical look, or just relax. Architect: Clement Chen.

Inside the pullman studio

Floor-to-ceiling storage along the wall adjoining the garage and oversize drawers under the counter maximize the narrow work space. Fixed overhead lighting and adjustable table lamp supplement the skylight and north-facing window. Architect: David Raphael Singer.

Multipurpose studios

Multitalented people sometimes need multipurpose studios. The three studios on these pages illustrate ways to organize several art activities into a single work area.

The attic studio on this page — photographed from each end — provides space to pursue a number of artistic endeavors, plus a gallery furnished with many of the props used in the artist's work.

On the facing page, two studios closely integrated with living areas illustrate how ample storage space and work surfaces can serve many purposes.

This end for acrylics
Light pouring in from skylight and window makes this end of the attic studio ideal for painting. White ceiling reflects light for further brightness. Vertical racks, painted a jolly orange, hold frames and canvases. Table to left is used for constructing collages. Design: Rae Abraham.

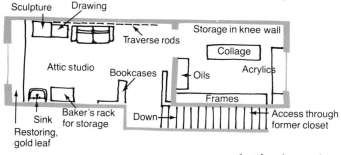

Art in the attic
Amidst a delightful hodgepodge of antiques and amusing props, the artist uses this portion of a long, narrow attic for sketching, water colors, and gold leafing. Paintings can be easily moved or changed along a traverse curtain rod mounted on the low, paneled wall. Fluorescent tubes installed in the ceiling's peak supplement natural light from skylight. Design: Rae Abraham.

Space for drawing, painting, sewing—plus

Part of a remodeled master bedroom suite, this multipurpose studio has three main work surfaces, each with its own storage area. There's a drafting table for drawing and painting (its storage is on left wall, shown in floor plan); a sewing counter with storage shelf above, cabinet below; and a work counter for matting and framing with storage above and below. Closet door to right leads to projector room; darkroom is through the rear doorway. Pairs of track lights focus on key work areas. Flooring has rich patina of old tile pavers, but it's actually brown paper bags glued to concrete and coated with polyurethane. Architect: Ron Yeo.

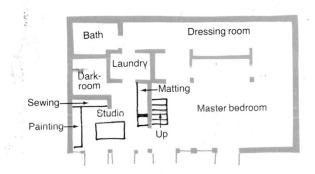

Craft room for the whole family

Everyone in the household enjoys this multifunction arts and crafts area. Supplies are stored in baskets on open shelves and under work counter. Handy sink is excellent for quick cleanups. Pass-through lets you enjoy the view through the family room's glass doors when you're seated at the counter. Architect: Brent Dickens.

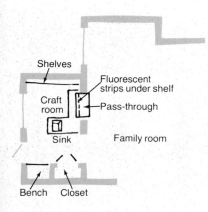

On the main floor

Radiant craft room, lighted by row of globes on ceiling joist and spotlights over sink, contains cabinetry recycled from an old chemistry lab. The owners painted the cabinets cheery red and fitted them with brightly colored knobs. Studio is used for ceramics, sculpture, and any craft that captures a family member's fancy.

At the bottom of the stairs

Graceful spiral staircase leads you into sunken entertainment area for a relaxing moment with friends. On one corner of the playhouse is a bay window that's as extraordinary as the rest of the structure—it has five sides.

Up in the loft

Private office is sequestered in upper region of loft. Slit of skylight, a window, and track lights illuminate the area. Floor lamp and antique wheelchair make an unconventional reading site.

Double-decker playhouse for crafts... & much more

Viewed from outside
Cedar shingles, diagonally placed external cedar plywood, plus the unusual bay windows, make the outside of the playhouse as interesting as the inside. Approximately 950 square feet, the whole structure revels in natural woods and unusual windows.

You name it, and there's a place for it in this treasure-packed two-story "playhouse."

A hide-away loft for leisure, weaving, and sewing dominates the top floor, with a side section outfitted as an office with desk and file cabinets. Peer over the custom-designed, iron-pipe spiral staircase and you'll look down on a gleefully busy studio for ceramics, sculpture, and more crafts. Next to it, there's a sunken lounge area for entertaining and displaying more art and collectibles. Accessible through the studio—but with an entry of its own—is the handsomely appointed library that appears on page 55.

Truly multipurpose and a fitting environment for a creative family, the playhouse is a marvel of natural woods, earth-tone tiles, and surprise corners filled with rustic antiques and amusing collectibles.

Architect: Sigrid Rupp.

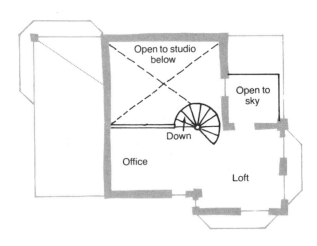

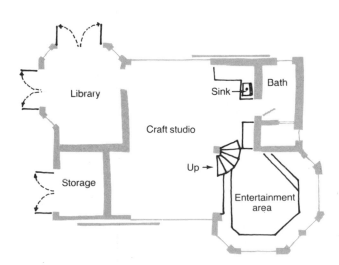

Work tables with a difference

A wobbly work table makes for wobbly workmanship, and a small, cramped, wobbly work table is practically worthless. Ranging from very simple to rather complex, the five tables shown here offer good ideas for work surfaces worthy of your art or craft.

When building one of these tables, remember to adjust the proportions to suit your height, if necessary. A waist-high work surface is best if you're standing.

If the project ideas on these pages look too difficult, there's always the tried-and-true work table made from a solid-core door mounted on four legs or two filing cabinets. Avoid hollow-core doors and lightweight filing cabinets for a table that has to hold anything heavy.

For further ideas on work tables, see the *Sunset* books, *Easy-to-Make Furniture* and *Easy-to-Make Tables & Chairs.*

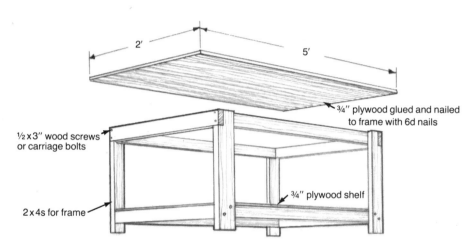

¾" plywood glued and nailed to frame with 6d nails

½ x 3" wood screws or carriage bolts

¾" plywood shelf

2 x 4s for frame

Simple, sturdy work table

Cross-braced legs and a top of at least 3/4-inch plywood or particle board make this work table solid enough for a workshop or hard-working studio. Top should be perfectly level (check it with a carpenter's level); you can fit lag bolts into the bottoms of the legs to compensate for an uneven floor. A splashboard fitted along the back side will keep small supplies from falling off. If you'll use this table in a workshop, nail a yardstick or tape measure to the front for measuring lumber.

Work table top is self-healing

For drawing and light work, you can use a flawed, hollow-core door "second" for a table top and hide the blemishes with architectural drafting "linoleum." This kind of linoleum seems to heal itself when cut with a knife or razor but is hard and smooth enough for drawing. Art, architectural, and engineering supply stores sell it in standard drafting-board sizes or by the yard. Cut the linoleum 1/2 inch smaller than door's perimeter and attach it with two-sided tape or contact cement. Architect: Michael Canatsey.

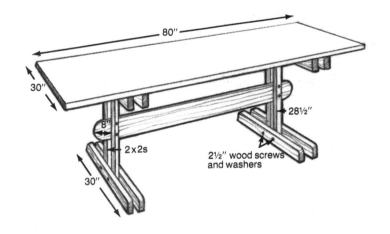

80"

30"

28½"

8"

30"

2 x 2s

2½" wood screws and washers

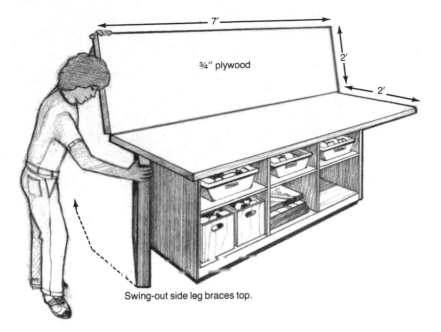

7'

¾" plywood

2'

2'

Swing-out side leg braces top.

Folding top for crafts or table tennis

Thanks to a piano hinge running the length of two hollow-core, 24-inch-wide doors, you can fold this table top in half and use it for crafts, or open it wide to support a piece of hardboard for table tennis. Plastic laminate protects edges of doors and the work surface when top is folded over. Side legs swing out to support fully opened top. Partitioned storage shelf below holds plastic bins for craft supplies, games. Design: Richard S. Robinson.

Sawhorse craft table

This versatile craft table is held together by dowels and glue. Sash chains change separation of sawhorse legs, so you can change its height to suit your project, then fold it away when you're through. Plywood top and storage shelf rest on sawhorse dowels. Design: Don Vandervort.

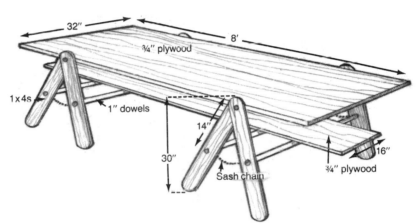

32"

8'

¾" plywood

1 x 4s

1" dowels

14"

30"

Sash chain

16"

¾" plywood

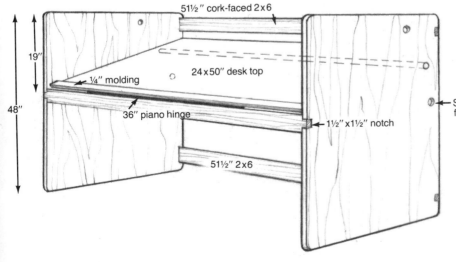

51½" cork-faced 2 x 6

19"

48"

¼" molding

24 x 50" desk top

36" piano hinge

1½" x 1½" notch

51½" 2 x 6

Slide dowel in lower holes for flat work surface.

Tilt-top drawing table

Hinged top can be tilted for sketching or drawing, lowered flat for water colors or writing. The table top rests on a long dowel that can be placed in lower or higher holes. (The concept is like the tilting back of a Morris chair.) A 36 to 48-inch piano hinge, held in place with wood screws, allows the top to tilt. Glue (or finishing nails) and 1/4-inch flathead brass screws hold the table together. Design: David Fitch.

Spaces for sewing

If you cut material in the kitchen, sew in the dining room, then have to run upstairs to view the results in a full-length mirror, you'll appreciate the efficiency of having complete sewing facilities in one room.

Besides the machine, a fully equipped sewing room includes a large work table for pinning patterns and cutting material, good light, a full-length mirror, storage space, and an ironing board. But you don't need a large room to sew in comfort. Many of the storage ideas on these pages can be adapted to limited space.

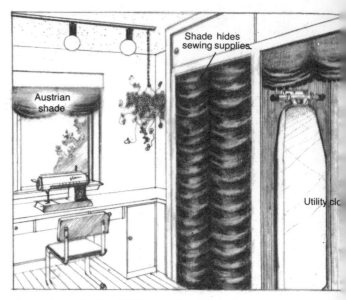

Austrian shades hide sewing closet

Pull up the gracefully scalloped Austrian shades and you'll find a double storage closet: one side holds sewing supplies and fabric, the other houses the ironing board. There's more storage overhead behind the sliding doors. Design: Barbara Namian.

Sewing center in a closet

Open the closet, lower the table, slide out the machine—and you're ready to sew. The 12-inch-deep closet houses a 2 by 4-foot table that swings down from its hiding place on a piano hinge (the legs are also attached to piano hinges). A 2-foot fluorescent strip lights the compact sewing center. Spools and scissors hang on 2-inch wood dowels glued into pegboard. Fabric, patterns, notions are stored on shelves above and below the table. Architect: William Boehm.

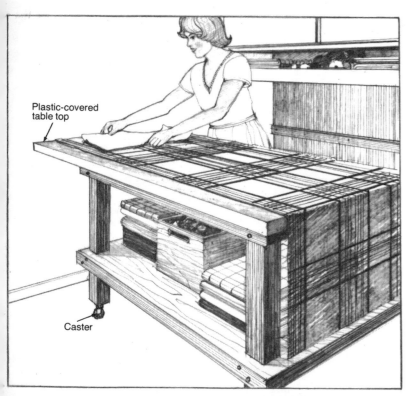

Roll out the work table

Perfect for pinning patterns or cutting fabric, the plastic-covered 36 by 69-inch table top sits on a heavy frame with a plywood shelf below for storage. Mounted on pivoting casters, the table rolls out from under a storage cabinet; back in place, it becomes a utility desk. Design: Arn Ghigliazza.

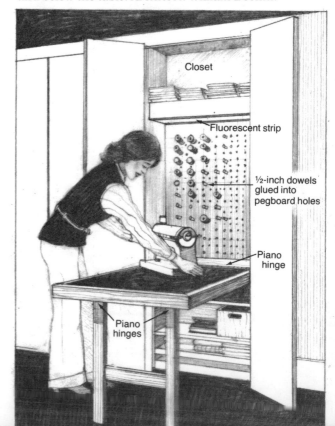

A place for everything

From notions stored in clear plastic containers to material hung on a fabric rack, everything the seamstress needs is easily found in the storage cabinet or walk-in closet. Built-in ironing board is handy for pressing seams and finished garments. Half-bath has door on other side leading to study.
Architect: Paul Zimmerman.

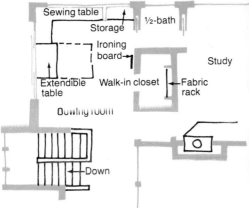

Enough work surface to spread out

And enough storage to put everything away—that's the result of good planning in this sewing room. Work table folds away when not in use. Besides the large storage cabinet, there's a rack for patterns above the sewing table. Pendant light and wall mounted light above sewing table supplement natural light from wall windows and clerestory window.
Architect: Paul Zimmerman.

Workshop ideas

A workshop can be a corner in the garage or a spectacular separate structure like the dream workshop on the facing page. No matter the size or location of your workshop, you'll want to pay special attention to four major features: workbench, storage, lighting, and electrical systems.

Your workbench should be the focus of the shop; wherever it's located the bench should be rock-solid for stability. Make sure the top is about waist high, so you can stand and work without fatigue.

Storage—like the layout of equipment—should be planned around a logical sequence of events, with frequently used supplies within easy reach. If you're right-handed, lumber storage would be somewhere to the left; tools for sawing, cutting, and drilling in the middle; and supplies for sanding and other finishing work to the right.

You'll want good overall artificial lighting to supplement any natural light and for work at night and on overcast days. Strong spot illumination is necessary for close work and for hazardous areas such as saw tables. Avoid light that throws shadows or creates glare. Four-foot-long double-tube industrial fluorescent fixtures are good for overhead lighting. For close work, single-tube fixtures can be installed beneath wall cabinets or on the wall behind a workbench. Adjustable spotlights mounted above power tools can direct light where you need it.

Electrical outlets should be close to wherever you use power tools. Avoid trailing cords; use spring-loaded cord retractors, if overhead outlets are necessary. For large power tools, provide at least one 20-amp circuit that's separate from the normal lighting circuits. Know your house's circuit capacity and the power draw of your tools; safety dictates that your tools should draw no more than 80 percent of circuit capacity. A key-operated master safety switch is an excellent idea, if children have access to your workshop.

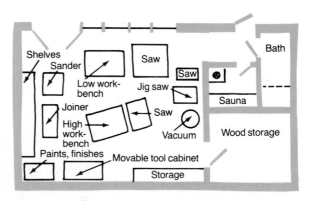

Workshop with cushioned flooring

Former garage was remodeled to hold workshop, supply and storage room, plus sauna and bath. Resilient flooring makes standing more comfortable. Fluorescent fixtures augment natural light from skylights and French doors. As safety feature, each electrical socket has its own circuit breaker. Design: Chris Payne.

Dream workshop

Elegant scissor trusses create large, open workshop without supports or posts. High, opaque plastic windows send in abundant natural light, supplemented by fluorescents. Open shelves and under-counter storage extend along a wall. Design: Edmund A. Stiles.

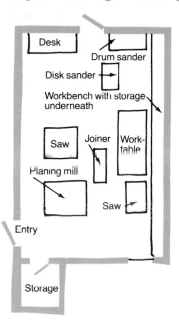

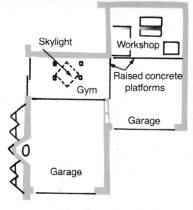

Platform workshop

Concrete 4-1/2-inch-high platform at end of garage is stage for an efficient workshop. Modular, wall-mounted strip with outlets every 15 inches provides ample power wherever needed. Key-operated master switch controls outlets, so kids can't play with equipment. White pegboard and white ceiling magnify natural light from skylight and the open garage door, so the fluorescents are rarely needed. See page 42 for photograph of mini-gym portion of garage. Architect: R. Gary Allan.

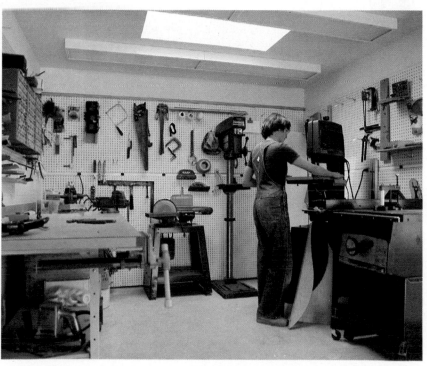

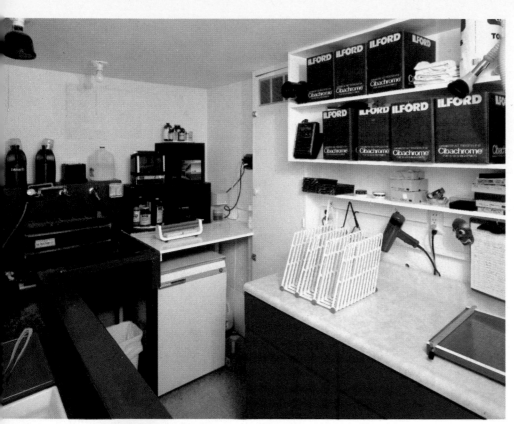

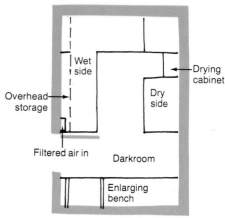

Basement darkroom

This 7-1/2 by 13-foot basement darkroom is easy to work in. There are no windows to worry about; the concrete slab, cushioned by vinyl flooring, means no vibrations; and natural insulation keeps room temperature even. Wet area has large, home-built fiberglass sink with several spigots and tray storage beneath. Dry side includes timer-set drying cabinet made with a hair dryer in bottom and a furnace filter. See floor plan for location of enlarging bench. Kitchen-style exhaust fan takes dust out of the room and brings in fresh, filtered air. Small TV screen above wet work counter is covered with orange acrylic sheet for safe watching. Design: Rob Super.

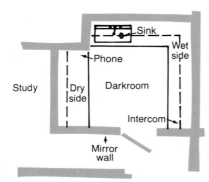

Den darkroom

Gentle pressure on the mirrored door reveals a darkroom, once a small den. The former wet bar now provides water for the wet side of the darkroom. Weatherstripping around door and wood strip on floor block out light. Room is air conditioned and equipped with intercom and telephone so photographer won't have to leave at a critical moment. Design: Ted Mintz.

Darkroom ideas

You can develop pictures almost anywhere—in a closet, bathroom, kitchen, converted den, or extra bedroom. Wherever you put your darkroom, the basic necessities remain the same: it has to be lightproofed, with "safelights" installed that won't harm prints; it should be well ventilated; vibrations and potential interruptions should be minimal; equipment should be arranged in order of use; storage should be ample. Running water in the room makes the printing process easier, though it's possible to have a "dry" darkroom and carry water trays of prints to another room for washing.

Ideally, the size of your darkroom is dictated by the size of the prints you want to make and the amount of equipment you own or hope to own. However, most people have to fit darkroom facilities into existing space. Spaciousness, fortunately, is no virtue in a darkroom; a large room means more steps between work stations and it's usually harder to keep dark and dust-free.

The most efficient arrangement is to place the sink and wet work area on one side of the room, dry counter on the other, with a small aisle in between. If there isn't enough space for an aisle, the developer tray should be partitioned from the enlarger to prevent accidental splashing.

Right-handed photographers probably will want to place equipment so work flows from left to right; left-handed people may prefer to work from right to left. The important thing is to keep the equipment in order of work flow.

Making color prints doesn't require a more elaborate darkroom, just total darkness while exposing the print. Even most safelights are too bright. However, once the enlarging exposure is over and the prints are placed in a light-tight drum for processing, the rest of the steps can be done in as much light as you want. You can buy lightproof cloth "tents" that fit over the enlarger, so color processing can take place at a kitchen or bathroom sink.

Chemical storage needs special attention. Unmixed chemicals can be left in their original containers. Half-used containers of developer or fixative are best stored in a childproof place outside the humid darkroom. Mixed chemicals should be stored close to where you'll use them and in clearly marked, nonreactive, airtight containers.

Floor plans on this page suggest darkroom arrangements for moderate, small, and closet-size areas.

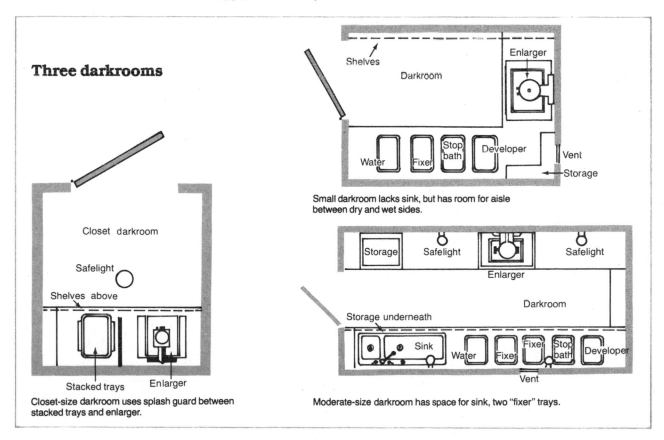

Three darkrooms

Shelves

Darkroom

Enlarger

Water | Fixer | Stop bath | Developer

Vent

Storage

Small darkroom lacks sink, but has room for aisle between dry and wet sides.

Closet darkroom

Safelight

Shelves above

Stacked trays   Enlarger

Closet-size darkroom uses splash guard between stacked trays and enlarger.

Storage | Safelight | Safelight

Enlarger

Darkroom

Storage underneath

Sink | Water | Fixer | Fixer | Stop bath | Developer

Vent

Moderate-size darkroom has space for sink, two "fixer" trays.

Index

Photographs

Edward B. Bigelow: 14 bottom, 19 bottom, 22 top and middle, 27 bottom, 28, 29, 30, 33, 34, 41, 48 top, 50, 63 bottom, 67 top, 69 bottom, 76 bottom, 77 top, 84, 85 bottom, 93 top. **Clyde Childress:** 14 top, 56 bottom, 75, 76 top, 78 top, 92. **Alyson Smith Gonsalves:** 91 top. **Steve W. Marley:** 5, 11, 12 bottom, 13 top, 19 top, 20, 21, 27 top, 47, 49 top, 57 top, 58 bottom, 64 top, 68 bottom, 78 bottom, 83 top. **Jack McDowell:** 3, 6, 12 top, 13 bottom, 22 bottom, 40, 42, 48 bottom, 49 bottom, 55, 56 top, 57 bottom, 58 top, 63 top, 64 bottom, 67 bottom, 68 top, 69 top, 70, 77 bottom, 83 bottom, 85 top, 86, 91 bottom, 94 bottom, back cover. **Rob Super:** 94 top. **Darrow M. Watt:** 39.